LEARNING
EDUCATIONAL APPLICATIONS

LEARNING
EDUCATIONAL APPLICATIONS

Walter B. Kolesnik

University of Detroit

ALLYN AND BACON, INC.   BOSTON • LONDON • SYDNEY

To Kathryn

Library of Congress Cataloging in Publication Data

Kolesnik, Walter Bernard, 1923-
    Learning, educational applications.

    Bibliography: p.
    Includes index.
    1. Learning, Psychology of. I. Title.
LB1051.K724   370.15'2   75-38652

ISBN 0-205-05443-9

Second printing . . . July, 1979

Contents

Preface

The purpose of this book is to explain as clearly and concisely as possible how learning takes place and how it can be facilitated. The book is introductory and nontechnical in nature, presuming no previous course work in education or psychology. It is intended primarily for beginning or prospective teachers in professional education courses; secondarily for those who will be teaching nonprofessionally, as parents or in some other capacity; and thirdly, as a refresher for more advanced students in the areas of education or psychology. The book touches upon informal learning in everyday life in the home and the community, but its main emphasis is on the kinds of learning that are expected to take place in schools.

The concepts of learning and teaching cannot, of course, be readily separated. Although this is hardly a methods book, each chapter includes some practical suggestions for teachers. Chapters 6, 8, and 10 focus on teaching. The rest of the book centers around various ways of learning and factors that affect the teaching-learning process. The suggestions offered to teachers and the orientation of the book as a whole reflects an integration of programming and discovery strategies as discussed in my *Humanism and/or Behaviorism in Education* (Allyn and Bacon, 1975).

I have tried to produce a book about learning that undergraduates would find reasonably interesting, useful, and informative, easy to read, related to their experiences, and addressed directly to them. Hence, the rather casual, conversational style, the numerous examples of concepts and principles under discussion, and the rather frequent use of first and second person pronouns.

This book is not intended as a substitute for any of the excellent comprehensive textbooks available on theories of learning, methods of teaching, or general educational psychology. It was designed for use in classes whose instructors prefer to have their students read a few shorter books rather than one lengthy text. Thus, there is no pretense that this book exhausts the subject of learning. It does not, for example, contain any detailed accounts of experimental studies in the area, encyclopedic summaries of research findings, or penetrating analyses of learning theories. It does, however, provide readers with an overview of several aspects of learning that they can use in understanding their own behavior, in guiding the learning of others, and as an introduction to more advanced study of teaching and learning.

WALTER B. KOLESNIK

1

An Overview of Learning

To live is to grow, to develop, to change. You will always be you, of course, because the basic core of your personality, your identity, your self, remains constant. But whatever you were like yesterday—to say nothing of last year—today you are somehow different: a little older, just a bit wiser perhaps, or at least better informed. Maybe you are a little less anxious or more self-confident. Maybe you are happier or more understanding, or more something or less something else. But somehow you are not exactly the same as you used to be. Although a few of the day-to-day changes that we undergo occur with dramatic suddenness, most of them are so gradual and minute as to be imperceptible. But they still happen.

LEARNING AND TEACHING

Some of the changes that characterize our lives are due, at least in part, to the unique set of genes which we have inherited as individual human beings and which differentiate us from every other human being. Some are due to innate drives or tendencies which we share with every other member of the human race. Some are due to the particular culture in which we have been raised or the particular environment in which we presently find ourselves.

Some of the things we do may be attributed to our temporary physiological condition, or to the level of social, emotional, intellectual, or physical maturation we have attained. Some might be consequences of factors that we are presently unaware of or do not fully understand, that no one perhaps will ever fully understand. Much of our behavior is undoubtedly due to a combination of factors and circumstances. But most of what we do—or know or think or feel or believe or would like to do—is the result of the process known as learning.

LIVING AND LEARNING

The term *learning,* as used here, refers to those changes in our behavior that result from our contacts with our environment and our interactions with other people. We begin to learn shortly after birth, and possibly before. Unless there is some serious physiological impairment, we continue to learn for as long as we live. To learn is to change, and to change is to live.

In addition to the knowledge we acquire, retain, and apply in our everyday lives, most of our social, intellectual, and psychomotor skills are learned. So are our values and attitudes, our beliefs and aspirations. Our fears, worries, and anxieties are learned. So are our interests and inclinations, our preferences and prejudices, our means of self-expression and our methods of self-control. Our adjustment patterns, our personality traits, our moral standards, and our ways of relating to other people, as well as our concepts of who we are, where we are headed, and how we will get there—all of these are what psychologists call learned responses.

Thus, learning is not, as is sometimes supposed, synonymous with schooling. It is, rather, coextensive with living.

INFORMAL LEARNING

Some of the most important things we know were not learned in school, nor were they specifically taught in school, nor for that matter were they systematically taught anywhere else. Rather, they were learned informally, casually, perhaps incidentally and maybe even accidentally from our parents or relatives, friends or acquaintances, from news or entertainment media, from clergymen or salesmen, or from various other individuals or institutions.

From informal educational agencies such as these we have learned, for example, how to walk and talk, how to feed and dress ourselves, what to eat and what to wear, what we mean by happiness, what we *can* do to achieve happiness, and what we *must* do for our very survival. It is largely through our everyday non-school experiences that we have learned, or are still in the process of learning, what the world is like, and what life is all about.

Chances are that our political views and our religious beliefs, our positions on various social issues, our attitudes toward and perceptions of other people, and our moral standards are not so much a consequence of our schooling as they are things we learned from our parents or friends. In all probability, television, magazines and newspapers, films and records have been at least as instrumental as school teachers and textbooks in shaping our values, tastes, and aspirations. Whom we associate with, what we talk about, how we spend our leisure time, how we spend our money, and the proverbial million-and-one specific things we do in the course of a day are more directly attributable to non-school than to school-related learning experiences.

I am not, of course, attempting to minimize the role of the school with respect to learning. I am, rather, trying to emphasize the point that much of our most significant learning takes place in casual, relatively unstructured, everyday situations outside the school. In these days when so very much seems to be expected of the schools and when schools are so frequently and vehemently denounced for their alleged failures, I think it is well worth noting that what or how much or how well a child learns in school depends to a very great extent on what he has learned or is learning or has failed to learn elsewhere, particularly in his home

HELPING OTHERS LEARN

While parents are undoubtedly the most important teachers that children will ever have, they cannot accomplish the task of education alone. This, of course, is why we have schools. Societies establish and maintain schools and require young people to attend them in order to help them learn things that they otherwise would not learn, or would not learn as well. Presumably the intended outcomes of schooling have something to do with the welfare of individual students as well as the preservation of society itself. While schools and colleges are by no means absolutely necessary for learning, the assumption underlying their existence is that they can and should facilitate learning, or make it more effective or efficient.

Perhaps you already are or someday will be professionally employed as a teacher. If so, you must recognize that the main job of a teacher at any level, from the nursery through graduate school, is to help people learn. Longer, more complex and highly technical definitions of teaching are readily available, but for our present purposes I should like to have us think of it as the process of guiding (or directing or facilitating) another person's learning.

Just as everyone is a learner whether he is enrolled in a school or not, so is everyone (well, almost everyone) a teacher, whether or not he is professionally certified as such. No matter what your occupation or marital status might be, chances are that you will spend a considerable portion of your time and energy in the years to come explaining something to someone or trying to persuade them to do or want or believe something.

Whether you will have children of your own to teach, or whether you will be teaching Brownies or Little Leaguers, or whether you will be teaching your employees or co-workers or prospective customers or clients or patients or friends or neighbors or fellow committee members, I do not know. But I am quite sure that somehow you will be adding to other peoples' stores of knowledge, influencing their attitudes, values, or beliefs, or somehow trying to help them change their behavior. In short, you will be teaching.

This book is primarily intended for young people who are preparing for careers as professional teachers—who will, in other words, be employed in those specially-prepared learning environments called schools. But it is also intended to serve those who will be teaching "informally" in non-school situations.

THE STUDY OF LEARNING

Since learning is practically synonymous with living, since all of us are constantly learning, and since most of us will spend a significant portion of our lives helping others learn, it would seem to follow that the nature of the learning process is a subject well worth investigating. To help others learn, professionally or otherwise, we need some understanding of what learning is, how it takes place, and how it can be facilitated. An understanding of learning is no less important for attainment of an understanding of ourselves and own own everyday behavior.

For literally thousands of years, philosophers have speculated on the question of how the mind works and whether there is indeed such a "thing" as a "mind." It was not until well into the nineteenth century, however, that psychology began to emerge as a science, and empirical, experimental methods were systematically employed to study learning, thinking, and other forms of human behavior and development. Since the 1890s, literally thousands of painstaking psychological research studies have been conducted under carefully controlled laboratory conditions, often with the aid of highly refined statistical techniques to verify the significance of their findings.

In the pages that follow, we will not go into any detail on the methodologies of these studies, nor will we concern ourselves with the specific facts and figures they have yielded. More specialized books that do so are readily available. We shall, however, be drawing extensively on the general conclusions of psychological research. We will be particularly concerned with the application of those conclusions and the corresponding principles of learning to the day-to-day job of teaching.

In addition to the specific data it has yielded concerning particular variables that affect learning, the scientific study of the learning process (or processes) has led to the formulation of several theories of learning. But before considering these theories, we should recognize an important distinction between learning as a process and the products in which it results.

PRODUCTS AND PROCESSES

The products of learning refer to the *what* of the learning experience; the process to the *how* of the experience itself. The products of learning, in other words, are the outcomes, the results, the things learned, the knowledge or skills or appreciations or whatever that the teacher aims at and tries to bring about. Ordinarily, the desired products of learning are specified or at least implied in the teacher's statement of objectives. The processes are the ways or means or methods by which these products are attained.

This book is primarily concerned with the learning processes. It deals, in short, not so much with what people learn or should learn, but *how* they learn. In actuality, the products and processes of learning cannot be separated. We cannot simply learn. We can only learn something. So the distinction that has just been made is more a matter of emphasis than anything else. But before proceeding much further with the processes, let's briefly consider the kinds of products that result from learning.

The outcome of learning is always a change in the learner's behavior. As a consequence of the learning process he acts or is able to act in a new way. These behavioral changes are not, of course, restricted to physical acts. They include what and how a person feels, believes, values, and knows, as well as what he does overtly. If there is no change in the behavior of the individual, no learning has taken place. If a student leaves a class at 11:50 with no more knowledge or skill than he had at 11 o'clock, and with precisely the same attitudes, etc., it is doubtful that he learned anything during the preceeding 50 minutes.

After a person has learned to spell or multiply or speak French or drive a car he is, in a sense, a different person—a fuller person—than he had previously been. He now can do something that he was previously incapable of doing, or of not doing as well. But the changes that result from the learning process are not always or necessarily improvements. Errors, bad habits, faulty attitudes, unsocial behavior and the like are also learned even though they are not intentionally taught.

OUTCOMES OF CLASSROOM LEARNING

The main outcomes of scholastic learning are ordinarily classified as cognitive, affective, or psychomotor. Cognitive learning pertains to the acquisition, retention, and application of knowledge, facts, information, principles, generalizations, meaning, understanding, etc. It is essentially intellectual in nature. Affective learning is more emotional. It refers to the formation of values, attitudes, likes and dislikes, feelings, prejudices, appreciations, etc. Psychomotor learning involves the acquisition or development of skills requiring neuromuscular coordinations, manual dexterity, the manipulation of objects or material, or some other form of physical activity.

Gym, shop, typing, drafting, and a few other classes might be particularly concerned with psychomotor outcomes; so might music and art classes when the emphasis is on performance. When the emphasis is placed on music or art appreciation, however, the intended outcomes are of the affective variety. Affective learning might be particularly important in literature or social studies classes where an attempt is made to develop certain values or attitudes, but just about any subject area can include the affective dimension. By and large, however, our elementary and high schools, colleges, and universities are primarily devoted to cognitive outcomes.

TAXONOMY OF EDUCATIONAL OBJECTIVES

The intended products as well as the processes of learning are inextricably connected with the objectives of the learning experience. What a teacher teaches and how she teaches it depend, in other words, on what she hopes to accomplish or what she expects her students to learn. In the mid-1950s a committee headed by Benjamin Bloom undertook the task of describing and distinguishing among the various cognitive objectives that were being used in our schools. The result was the now famous and still widely-used taxonomy, or classification, of educational objectives. The committee subsequently produced taxonomies in the affective domain.

THE COGNITIVE DOMAIN

Bloom and his associates identified six levels of learning outcomes in the cognitive domain, the first having to do with knowledge and the other five with intellectual skills and abilities.

Level one objectives expect the student to "know"—meaning here to be able to recall—specific facts, definitions, principles, etc. This level corresponds approximately to rote memorization, but there are gradations or degrees of complexity ranging from knowledge of word meanings to knowledge of abstract theories. Still, the knowledge referred to here presumes no deep insights and is of the type that can easily be measured on a multiple-choice test.

Level two objectives pertain to comprehension. That is what the taxonomists regard as a step above mere memorization, but still as the lowest level of understanding. This level includes translation, interpretation, and extrapolation. Here the student is expected to be able to restate material in his own words or to use that material but without necessarily seeing its full implication.

Level three objectives involve application. Here the student is expected to apply his knowledge in concrete situations. He must, of course, remember and understand the material but is expected to go a step further and put that knowledge to use.

Level four objectives have to do with analysis. This requires a higher level of understanding than step two. At this level, the student is expected to break material down into its component parts, demonstrate that he grasps the relationships between these parts, and that he recognizes the structure or organizing principle that holds them together.

Level five objectives involve synthesis, the opposite of analysis. Here the student is expected to put together the parts or pieces or elements of what he has learned, to organize or relate them in such a way that new insights or deeper or fuller understandings result.

Level six objectives pertain to evaluation. Here the student is expected to make a value judgment about the material he has learned, either in terms of criteria which he is given or which he himself has formulated. This level corresponds to what we shall be discussing in Chapter 5 as critical thinking.

THE AFFECTIVE DOMAIN

The first level of objectives in the affective domain, according to the taxonomy, is receiving or attending. At this level, the student is sensitive to or aware of stimuli having emotional overtones. He is open to new experiences, does not attempt to avoid them, and at least takes notice of them.

Level two is responding. Here the student goes beyond simply accepting, attending to, or tolerating new ideas or experiences. He actively commits himself, at least in a small way, to behaving in a new way. He voluntarily engages in a new course of action and derives at least a small degree of personal satisfaction from doing so.

Level three is valuing. At this level, the learner demonstrates that he recognizes the worth of an object or a behavior pattern. His behavior is motivated not simply by a desire to comply or conform, but by a rather firm conviction that certain standards, views, or ideas are better than others.

Level four is organizing. Here the learner relates his values to each other, establishes a hierarchy or priorities among them, and begins developing a value "system."

Level five is called "characterization by a value or value complex." What this means is that at this level the learner acts consistently in accordance with the value system he has internalized, while remaining open to the possibility of further revising that system. Moreover, he integrates his beliefs, ideas, attitudes, etc. into a "world view" or his own philosophy of life.

THE PSYCHOMOTOR DOMAIN

The original taxonomy committee has not as yet formulated objectives in the psychomotor domain. Kibler and his associates,

THE MAJOR TYPES OF EDUCATIONAL OBJECTIVES

Cognitive Domain	Affective Domain
6.0 Evaluation	
5.0 Synthesis	5.0 Value Complex
4.0 Analysis	4.0 Organizing
3.0 Application	3.0 Valuing
2.0 Comprehension	2.0 Responding
1.0 Knowledge	1.0 Receiving (attending)

however, have tentatively submitted the following classification:

The first level of objectives has to do with gross movements of the upper or lower limbs. These include activities involving the arms and shoulders, feet and legs, and a degree of coordination among them.

The second level pertains to finely coordinated movements of the hands and fingers, particularly in conjunction with the eyes or the ears or both.

The third level involves nonverbal communication. Here the student is expected to be able to use appropriate facial expressions, gestures, and bodily movements in order to convey some message or feeling.

The fourth level has to do with speech. At this level, the learner is able to produce meaningful sounds, to coordinate these sounds into meaningful words and messages, and to project these sounds along with nonverbal means of communicating so as to affect other people.

INCIDENTAL LEARNING

With respect to classroom learning, a distinction can be made between primary and incidental outcomes. Primary outcomes are the products which are desired by, aimed at, and intentionally worked for by the student or teacher or both. Any of the objectives in the taxonomy could be of this type. To read, to spell, to write shorthand, to solve mathematical problems, to play the piano, to appreciate poetry, to reject brutality are all examples of primary outcomes. Ordinarily, whatever a teacher says or thinks he is teaching, whatever a student thinks or says she is learning is stated in terms of what we are calling primary learning.

Incidental learning is casual, usually unintended, and is often a by-product or an accompaniment of primary learning. It takes place along with, and sometimes instead of, primary learning. During a reading lesson, for example, students might be learning some things other than how to read. They might, incidentally, be learning something about history or geography or science or sports, depending on what the story is about. They might be learning honesty or compassion or some other virtue that is brought out in the moral of the story.

During a math class, a student might be learning to like, or dislike, mathematics, or the teacher, or the school, or the authority structure that compels him to attend school and study math. During a science class, while the teacher is teaching the concept of lunar eclipses, the student might not be learning about lunar eclipses at all. He might instead be learning that science in general and astonomy in particular is a bore, or that he would not like to become an astronomer himself. He might be learning that he is brighter (or duller) than most of his classmates, or that his teacher cannot teach very well.

Incidental learning can be good, bad or neutral. Sometimes the outcomes of such learning are trivial or distracting, but they could turn out to be far more important in the life of the student than the primary material he is being formally taught. While "primarily" learning history, for example, a student might concomitantly be learning effective study habits, desirable school attitudes, or a love of learning in general. But he might also be learning that the main consideration in his history class is getting a good grade and that the end justifies the means in his doing so.

THE HIDDEN CURRICULUM

A great deal of incidental learning results from what has been called the "hidden" curriculum. This term refers to outcomes of learning which are not indicated in course syllabi or lesson plans, which the teacher does not formally teach or intend to teach, which he might not even realize that his students are learning, and which might not even be true, but which his students do nevertheless acquire. Such material is not concealed maliciously or surreptitiously or even deliberately. Rather, it subtly insinuates itself into the regular curriculum without the teacher's awareness and is thus hidden from him as well as his students.

A good example of the hidden curriculum has to do with the learning of "sex role" stereotypes. For many years the stories and illustrations in elementary school readers have taught students—incidentally—that girls are clean, polite, and docile, while boys are aggressive, more inclined to get dirty, and have more fun; that

11

mommies change diapers and prepare meals while daddies do all sorts of mysterious things that are far more interesting and exciting; that girls cry, but boys do not; that girls are timid and dependent, boys courageous and self-reliant, etc.

Similarly, it has been charged, instructional materials and traditional white-oriented courses of study have contributed significantly, though perhaps inadvertently, to the perpetuation of certain racial and ethnic stereotypes. People of your parents' generation, for example, probably never saw a picture of a black person in any of their textbooks except perhaps as a servant, a slave, or an inhabitant of "uncivilized" Africa. They may have heard of George Washington Carver, but other than that, I doubt that they learned much about the contributions of black people to science, literature, or the arts. I hope that no one intentionally tried to teach them that black people "have never amounted to anything," but this is nevertheless a generalization that they might have learned.

Since the mid 1960s or thereabouts educators and textbook publishers, among others, have been conscious of the problems of the hidden curriculum and have attempted to deal with them through the introduction of new courses, new units of instruction, new instructional materials, etc. Many of these administration-based innovations have undoubtedly served useful purposes but in and of themselves they have not eliminated the problem, for the hidden curriculum often pertains not so much to what is taught or even implied but to how it is taught.

Through the hidden curriculum, for example, regardless of what appears in the official course of study, a student might acquire and retain the impression that he is stupid, or troublesome, or worthless, or bad, or a failure, or odd, or insignificant, or hopeless, or too dumb to bother with. Let us hope that he is not explicitly told these things, but even if he isn't, these might be among the messages he receives. Through the hidden curriculum, to take another example, the student might learn that regardless of what the teacher says about independent thinking, the safest thing for him to do when he disagrees with her is to keep his mouth shut.

THEORIES OF LEARNING

So far we have noted that learning is practically coextensive with living. Learning goes on all the time (maybe even while we are asleep) whether we are aware of it or not. Learning always results in a change in the learner's behavior, although the change is not always desired, nor is it necessarily an improvement nor is it necessarily permanent. We have also noted that the main function of a teacher—professional or otherwise—is to help people learn.

What does it mean to learn something? What happens when we learn? How does learning take place? What causes us to learn and to remember or forget what we have learned? Why do some people learn more readily than others? How can one person most effectively help another person to learn? To questions such as these, there are no easy answers. There are dozens of theories of learning, but none of them has anything apporaching universal acceptance.

TEACHERS AND PSYCHOLOGISTS

Theoretical questions about the nature of learning are ordinarily of more interest to psychologists than they are to classroom teachers. Some psychologists have devoted the better part of their adult lives to studying the process. They have attempted to formulate and verify principles or "laws" to account for all forms of learning, ranging from a dog's learning to stand on its hind legs and beg for food to a philosopher's learning the meaning of life. They continue to seek common elements in such apparently different kinds of learning experiences and have tried to devise a single theory to account for both. But they have yet to reach a set of conclusions about learning that is completely satisfactory to themselves, much less to their fellow psychologists. Still, the search goes on.

A teacher's main function is not to define learning or to explain how it occurs. His concern, rather, is with the more practical problems of guiding the student's learning activities whatever the nature of the learning process might be. Still, in order to carry out his responsibilities, a teacher needs at least tentative answers to the theoretical questions raised above. This is not to suggest that teachers need a profound understanding of the learning process or a systematic, comprehensive theory of learning that meets the rigorous standards of an experimental psychologist. But they do need some set of principles and assumptions on which to base their practices. Every teacher does, in fact, have at least an informal, loosely structured theory of learning, even if it is only based on old adages, conventional wisdom, and his own experiences.

VARIETIES OF THEORIES

When a teacher turns to psychology for information about the nature of learning, he is offered a choice of literally dozens of systematic theories. Among the better known of these are the following:

Bandura's theory of modelling and social learning

Bruner's theory of cognitive development

Estes's statistical theory of learning

Freud's psychoanalytical theory

Guthrie's continguity theory

Hull's systematic behavior theory

Lewin's topological theory

Mowrer's two-factor theory

Pavlov's classical conditioning theory

Piaget's theory of cognitive development

Skinner's operant conditioning theory

Thorndike's theory of connectionism

Tolman's sign theory

Wertheimer's gestalt theory

Wheeler's organismic theory

In addition to these, there are various information processing theories, neurophysiological theories, mathematical theories, instructional theories, theories of psychoeducational design, and Gagne's theory of types of learning. There are others that I have neglected or forgotten to mention.

Some of these theories, as their authors' readily concede, have little or no relevance to classroom instruction, nor are they intended to. They are offered as conclusions of, or hypotheses for, "pure" rather than applied psychology. In this book we shall not be concerned with theories of learning as such, but with some of their practical classroom applications. If you are interested in theory you might want to examine the Hilgard and Bower or Snelbecker books to which reference is made at the end of this chapter.

Those theories having the greatest and most direct implications for classroom learning can be grouped under two main headings: association and cognitive. These can be viewed as corresponding, at least in a general way, to behavioral and humanistic psychology respectively. The link between behaviorism and association theories of learning is particularly strong. Somewhat more tenuous is the relationship between humanism and cognitive theories.

Practically every method of teaching and pattern of curriculum organization can be justified in terms of one or another or a combination of these two systems. The same is true of most of the educational innovations that have been tried in recent years and reforms that are currently being proposed. Both of these "families" have their subdivisions, factions, and splinter groups. Thus, all of those who are classified as associationists, for example, are by no means in total agreement with one another on all details of the learning process. But their different views of the learning process do have enough in common to warrant being grouped and discussed together.

ASSOCIATION THEORIES

Association theories are so called because they attempt to explain all learning in terms of the formation and strengthening of connections between the stimuli acting on organisms and the responses they make accordingly. Some association theories, therefore, are referred to as connectionist or stimulus response (S-R) theories.

Association theories can be traced back at least as far as 400

B.C., when Aristotle pointed out that things which are contiguous or experienced together in time or space tend to become associated. So do experiences which are similar to or the opposite of one another. We tend to associate snow with coldness, for example, coldness with winter, winter with summer, etc. Much later in history such English empiricists as John Locke and Thomas Hobbes, among others, tried to explain memory, perception, reasoning and all other forms of mental activity in terms of associations or sequences of ideas. Like Aristotle, the eighteenth and nineteenth century empiricists are more properly regarded as philosophers than psychologists, but they did lay the foundations on which much of contemporary learning theory has been built.

Modern association theories of learning were formulated in the early twentieth century, largely through the efforts of Ivan Pavlov, John Watson, and Edward L. Thorndike. More recently their theories have been refined and revised by such behavioral psychologists as Clark Hull, Edwin Guthrie, and B.F. Skinner, all of whom explain learning in terms of some form of conditioning. The theories of Skinner, in particular, underlie the concepts of behavior modification, behavioral engineering, behavioral objectives, and programming, which we shall discuss in chapters 3, 6, and elsewhere.

COGNITIVE THEORIES

While association theories of learning center around the concepts of stimuli (such as those emanating from a teacher, a film, or a textbook) and responses made by the learner, cognitive theories stress the variables that intervene between the stimuli and the responses. Among these variables are the individual learner's purposes, aspirations, beliefs, ideals, and his existing store of knowledge as it is currently organized.

Cognitive theorists point out that two students are likely to respond quite differently to the very same stimuli because of what they have already learned, what they hope to achieve, what they feel they are capable of achieving, because of differences in the ways their minds work, or because of other differences which distinguish one person from another. Thus, according to cognitive theories, learning is a far more complex process than simply linking up connections between stimuli and responses. It is more of an individual matter involving perception, the processing and assimilation of information, the development of insights and the discovery of meaning.

Cognitive theories of learning can be ideologically related to humanistic psychology. Some of the key principles of humanistic psychology can be traced back to the humanism of classical antiquity and to the renaissance idea that the proper study of mankind is man. Modern humanistic psychology, however, did not emerge until the late 1940s. Differing as they do on a number of particulars, such humanistic psychologists as Abraham Maslow, Carl Rogers, and Arthur Combs emphasize what they regard as the distinctively human aspects of personality, such as the individual's uniqueness and capacity for self-determination.

Cognitive theories of learning, sometimes referred to as field theories, are derivatives or modifications of gestalt psychology. Gestalt psychology takes its name from the German word that means pattern or configuration. Gestalt psychology grew out of studies of perception conducted in the first quarter of the century by Max Wertheimer, Wolfgang Kohler, and Kurt Koffka. According to these gestaltists, a person's sensory "field" is always organized or structured in such a way that an object is always perceived as standing out against a background and in relationship to other objects or stimuli. The manner in which an individual perceives these relationships determines what he "sees" in a situation and what he does as a consequence.

Among those who have contributed significantly to the development of cognitive theories are Kurt Lewin, John Dewey, Jean Piaget, and Jerome Bruner. Just as associationists do not agree with one another on all of the particulars regarding the nature of the learning process, so are there differences of opinion among contemporary cognitive theorists. Still, they are generally agreed that learning occurs when we come to understand the basic structure or the pattern of relationships in a subject, when we recognize the relationships of parts to parts and of parts to the whole, when we reorganize our experiences and perhaps with a flash of intuition begin to perceive things in a new and more meaningful way. The way learning occurs, they believe, is essentially through a process of individual personal discovery.

17

In Chapters 4 and 6, we shall discuss discovery, perception, and some other implications of cognitive theories at greater length.

TWO VIEWS OF TEACHING

Association and cognitive theories agree in principle that the function of a teacher is to help people learn. But corresponding to the two basic theories of learning are two different, though not mutually exclusive, concepts of how this help should be given. Behavioral-association theories underlie that concept of the teacher as a classroom manager or a director of the learning process. Humanistic-cognitive theories are more consistent with the idea of the teacher as a kind of guide or a facilitator of learning. The former lends support to a systematic, carefully pre-planned expository or programming approach to teaching, while the latter is more compatible with flexible, spontaneous methods of teaching.

Association theories can be used to justify a classroom that is largely teacher-centered. Here, the students' interests, needs, goals, and problems are taken into account, and there might be a concerted effort at individualizing the instructional program. But by and large, the teacher decides which particular kinds of changes are to be brought about in his students, what they will learn, and what kinds of responses they will eventually come to make. Then he proceeds to plan, organize and direct the work of the class in such a way that the desired responses will be made.

The role of the teacher, according to cognitive psychology, is considerably broader than forming and strengthening connections or producing pre-planned responses. His function is to organize the learning situation so that significant relationships emerge and personal understanding of the material results. Insofar as possible, the learning experiences are structured so that the learner is able to discover and generalize these relationships for himself. The *how* of learning, or the process, is considered to be of greater importance than the *what*, or the product. A great deal of emphasis is placed on helping students "learn how to learn."

As we have seen, learning, to a cognitive theorist, is the student's personal discovery of meaning. If a teacher is to help a student make such discoveries, she must begin by trying to see the world—

and especially the subject matter she is teaching—through the eyes of the student. The teacher might be convinced that there are certain things that the child will need to know five or ten or twenty years later and she will want to guide him accordingly. The student, however, is likely to be much more concerned with the here and now than with the future. The cognitive-type teacher, therefore, attempts to perceive the child's existing situation as he does so that she can help make the material more meaningful to him in his present situation.

The vast majority of teachers and psychologists cannot be neatly categorized as behaviorists or humanists, as association or cognitive theorists. They are, rather, eclectic, selecting and adapting what they regard as the better features of each system. For certain types of learning, they might find that association theories offer more satisfactory explanations, and that methods of teaching based on those theories are likely to be most effective. For other kinds of learning, they might find cognitive theories and principles more promising. As a kind of middle-of-the-road moderate who likes to have his cake and eat it too, and who feels most comfortable living in the best of "both" psychological worlds, it is this type of eclectic, humanistic behavioral, cognitive *cum* association approach that I am inclined to recommend.

WAYS OF LEARNING

Although every theorist would not necessarily agree, we might note that there are (or at least seem to be) different ways of learning—each requiring a somewhat different method of teaching. A person does not learn to read, for example, in the same way that he learns to write, or play pinochle, or drive a motorcycle, or enjoy symphonies. Learning algebra is not quite the same process as learning to converse in Italian, or to use this rather than that brand of toothpaste, or to believe in God or to love one's neighbor. Learning where to get the best deal on a used car or who the "easy" professors are apparently involves a different process from learning who Alcibiades was or how to swim the backstroke.

As we shall see in the chapters ahead, certain types of learning are due at least in part to imitation. Others involve trial and error.

Some forms of learning can be readily explained in terms of conditioning. Others can be more readily explained in terms of discovery or perception. One way of learning some material is through conceptualization. Other ways are through inference, or problem solving, or critical or creative or reflective or reproductive thinking. Most of our learning experiences include more than one of these processes. Some might include all of them.

SUMMARY

Most human behavior is the result of learning. We begin learning shortly after birth, and possibly before. Ordinarily we continue learning until we die. Thus, learning is a much broader concept than schooling. Some of our most important learning occurs informally in situations outside the school. Whether or not you are attending a school or are professionally certified as a teacher, you will be spending a great part of your life learning and helping others to learn.

Schools are maintained in order to help people learn the kinds of things they want or need to learn, but that they otherwise could not learn or would not learn as well. There are differences of opinion as to precisely what these things are or should be. But the intended outcomes of classroom learning are commonly classified as cognitive, affective, or psychomotor. Cognitive objectives involve the acquisition of knowledge and the development of intellectual skills. Affective objectives pertain to emotionally-toned behavior, such as feeling, believing, and valuing. Psychomotor objectives include various types of physical activity.

In addition to the primary outcomes, students also learn many things in school "incidentally," by means of the "hidden curriculum." They learn, in other words, a number of things that are not intentionally taught, including their concepts of themselves and their attitudes toward school.

Literally dozens of theories of learning have been formulated. Some of them admittedly have little or no relevance to the work of the school. Those theories which have the greatest implications for classroom learning and instruction can be classified as association or cognitive. Association theories explain learning in terms of conditioning and support the concept of teaching as programming. Cognitive theories place the major emphasis on perception and underlie the use of discovery methods of teaching. These two kinds of teaching strategies, like the two basic theories of learning to which they are related, are not mutually exclusive. Most of the ideas and principles that are just briefly noted in this chapter are examined at greater length in the chapters ahead.

Recommended Readings

Bereiter, Carl. *Must We Educate?* Englewood Cliffs, N.J.: Prentice-Hall, 1973. A provocative book on the relationship between schools and education. Raises the question of whether education in the sense of one person's deliberately altering another is moral, necessary, or even desirable.

Bloom, Benjamin S. et al. *Taxonomy of Educational Objectives. Handbook I: Cognitive Domain.* New York: Longsman Green, 1956. Explains and gives examples of various kinds of cognitive objectives in each of the six major categories mentioned in this chapter. Shows how the taxonomy can be used in teaching, testing, and curriculum planning.

Clarizio, Harvey F. et al., eds. *Contemporary Issues in Educational Psychology.* 2d ed. Boston: Allyn and Bacon, 1974. A book of readings. The first three articles, by Robert Ebel, Weinstein and Fantini, and Carl Rogers, reflect three different viewpoints regarding the purposes of schools. The book also contains articles on each of the other subjects dealt with in the chapters ahead.

Hilgard, Ernest R., and Bower, Gordon H. *Theories of Learning.* 4th ed. Englewood Cliffs, N.J.: Prentice-Hall, 1975. Analyzes several of the more important theories of learning including those of Thorndike, Pavlov, Skinner, Piaget, and Freud, as well as gestalt, mathematical, and information processing theories. The last chapter deals with theory of instruction.

Kibler, Robert J. et al. *Objectives for Instruction and Evaluation.* Boston: Allyn and Bacon, 1974. Includes a clear discussion of, and practical

22

suggestions for using, objectives in the cognitive, affective, and psychomotor domains. Also related to chapter 6 of this book, where performance objectives are discussed.

Kolesnik, Walter B. *Humanism and/or Behaviorism in Education.* Boston: Allyn and Bacon, 1975. Compares humanism and behaviorism and shows how they can be synthesized for purposes of classroom instruction.

Krathwohl, David R. et al. *Taxonomy of Educational Objectives. Handbook II: Affective Domain.* New York: David McKay, 1964. Similar to the book by Bloom mentioned above, but centering around various kinds of objectives in the five affective categories.

Leichter, Hope J. "The Family as Educator." *Teachers College Record,* December, 1974. An introductory article in a special issue of this journal devoted to the role of the family in education. The issue includes articles by Margaret Mead, Urie Bronfenbrenner, and other noted authorities in the field.

Snelbecker, Glenn E. *Learning Theory, Instructional Theory, and Psychoeducational Design.* New York: McGraw-Hill, 1974. Similar in content to the Hilgard book, places more emphasis on theory of instruction and psychoeducational research and development.

2

Learning by
Imitation or
Trial and Error

Certain patterns of behavior are commonly found to "run in the family." Children often are found to resemble their parents not only in physical appearance but socially, emotionally, intellectually, and in other ways as well. These patterns and resemblances are sometimes attributed to heredity, but they are far more likely to be the result of imitation.

A "chip off the old block" does not inherit his father's interest in sports, for example, or his mother's love of music. Neither do parents genetically transmit such traits as shyness or aggressiveness, quick temper or patience, antisocial tendencies or neurotic symptoms. But there is a good chance (no certainty, of course) that sons and daughters will learn to act in these ways if their parents do, by means of imitation.

IMITATION

Imitation as a way of learning has been widely researched by social psychologists such as Albert Bandura, but it has not received nearly as much attention from educational psychologists as it deserves. By and large, educators have tended to disparage imitation as "mere copying," or as a process that militates against creativity. For reasons such as these, I am singling it out rather early in this book for special emphasis.

Very few, if any, learning experiences can be satisfactorily explained by imitation alone. There are, however, numerous kinds of cases that involve an element of imitation and can be at least partially explained in this way. Take, for example, the learning of language, on which so much subsequent learning depends.

LANGUAGE

In considering language, we must distinguish between two closely related but different abilities: the ability to use language correctly and effectively so as to convey ideas, and the ability to understand the messages we receive from others. Let's begin with the former. Psychologists and psycholinguists do not agree with one another or among themselves as to precisely how a child learns to speak his native language. But they do agree that it is a rather complex procedure involving a whole lot more than simple imitation. Still, the imitative aspect certainly does enter into the process to a marked degree.

The earliest babbling, gurgling, and cooing of the infant in random, meaningless fashion are probably unlearned physiological responses, often made involuntarily. But as casual observation reveals, by about two years of age the child is reproducing, or attempting to reproduce, deliberately and systematically some of the sounds he hears emanating from his parents, his pet, the television set or some other source. Maybe he is specifically urged to "Say 'daddy' " or to imitate his dog. ("What does the doggie say?") More commonly, without being prodded he just happens to use certain words—possibly including a few which his parents would rather he did not—that he has heard others use. Thus, in the early stages of linguistic development he learns, largely through imitation, to reproduce a variety of phonemes, to combine these into meaningful words, and words into simple sentences.

Imitation alone does not explain how children are able to

produce sentences that they have never heard nor does it explain certain other phenomena in the areas of language usage or linguistic development. As we shall see later, in any type of imitative behavior an element of trial and error as well as conditioning is likely to be found. Maturation or natural processes of growth and development as well as psychological readiness and reinforcement are among the other factors involved in the learning of a language and the formation of meaningful concepts. For the present, let us simply note that it is at least in part through imitation that a child learns not only pronunciation and vocabulary, accents and idioms, but also begins to acquire the rudiments of grammar and syntax.

Early in life the child begins to notice that by uttering certain sounds at the appropriate time, other people can cause certain things to happen. So he copies their vocal behavior in order to satisfy some of his desires or fill some of his needs. He discovers (that's another way of learning: through discovery) that when he says something remotely resembling "water," for example, he is given something to quench his thirst. Through further imitation—along with his own discoveries and other forms of learning that we will be discussing—he expands his vocabulary, improves his pronunciation, refines his grammar, and becomes progressively more articulate. In like manner, by copying the speech patterns of his associates, he might learn to speak a foreign language or a different dialect.

Before concluding this very brief discussion of language development, we should note that some of the most important work in this area has been done by Noam Chomsky, the founder of transformational grammar and one of our most influential psycholinguists. Chomsky believes that there are certain basic rules common to all languages and that human beings, by their very nature, have a genetic propensity for learning these rules. Thus, he vigorously denies that imitation, supplemented by reinforcement, is the primary means of learning a language. He maintaines, rather, that every child is preprogrammed to learn, not a specific language or dialect, but the general outlines or structure of language. Chomsky's theories are too technical and complex for us to pursue in this book, but if you are interested in this matter, you might want to check some of his writings. One of his books is included in the chapter bibliography.

READING AND LISTENING

Once a person has acquired the ability to understand a language, two of the most common ways he learns are through listening and reading. Both of these are largely, though not entirely, imitative processes. Let's take reading first.

Many (maybe most) of the things you learned in school beyond, say, the fifth or sixth grade were probably acquired through reading. I suspect that much of the knowledge, as well as many of the skills, attitudes, etc., that you acquired outside the school were also learned through reading. But note that when you read something attentively with the intention of remembering what you have read, you are in a very real sense imitating the author.

Whether it is a textbook, a newspaper, a set of directions on how to do something or whatever, when you read, in effect, you repeat or say to yourself what the author has written. You might question or even reject his message, but when he says, for example, "Freud was a neurotic," you respond by perhaps subvocally saying that Freud was a neurotic as the idea "passes through your mind." When you see a "No left turn" sign, you imitate the behavior of countless other drivers who refrain from turning left at that particular point. These behaviors can be more completely explained in terms of conditioning, which we will take up in the next chapter. For now, let's simply recognize that the total act of reading includes, among other things, an element of imitation.

The same is true of listening. When one of your teachers makes a statement, assuming of course that you are paying attention to what she says, you imitate her by making the same statement mentally, or perhaps by writing it down in your notebook. On next week's quiz, you might want to answer the questions very much as she has, or would have, answered them, maybe even using her exact words. Note that I have not said that this is good. All I am saying is that this kind of imitative response happens, and that it is one way we learn.

When we mention learning through listening we imply, of course, teaching through telling. Telling is probably how most teaching has always taken place in homes as well as in schools. In recent years, the telling method—better known at the college level as the lecture method—has not had a particularly good press. Articles or pronouncements in its favor are few and far between.

Far more fashionable, as perhaps they should be, are discussions, small group projects, individualized study, field experiences, independent research, and the like. At lower levels of the educational ladder, the telling or teacher-centered explaining method has also been subjected to a great deal of criticism.

I am by no means willing to undertake a defense of the lecture method or its elementary school counterpart as the best method of teaching. But I know of no more efficient way of teaching "content" to a great many people at the same time. Whatever the merits of learning by listening or by reading might be, we should note that most learning involves one or another or both, and that both include this element of imitation.

SKILLS

In addition to the role it plays in verbal or cognitive learning, imitation is also instrumental in the learning of psychomotor skills. It is, for example, to a great extent through imitation that the preschooler learns to use his toys appropriately, to play games and to perform stunts, to "help" his parents with simple domestic chores, to eat with a knife and fork, and to develop a variety of other skills commensurate with that stage of his development. Later, it is largely through imitation that he learns to print, write, draw, color, cut and paste, sing and dance, and for that matter to get into trouble. Although there is a lot more to it than that, as is the case with learning language, even the learning of reading skills involves an element of imitation. When, for example, a teacher points to a word or a letter, pronounces it, and expects the child to do the same, she might not be using the latest or the most sophisticated methodology, but she is certainly relying on the way of learning that is presently under discussion.

At least a bit of imitation also enters into learning to compute, to solve mathematical problems, to express one's thoughts on paper, to operate a typewriter, drive a car, build a bird house, etc. In all of these activities, demonstrations of how to do it or models to be followed are likely to be given. In so far as they involve skills or techniques, imitation enters into the learning of creative or expressive arts such as music and painting as well. This is why so many aspiring painters spend so much time in art galleries copying masterpieces, and why music students are encouraged to listen to the great performers in their fields.

Observation and imitation are important factors in learning athletic skills, such as the fine points of baserunning or blocking and tackling, and in learning psychomotor skills involving the use of tools or machinery. In short, it is largely, though not exclusively, through imitation that children—and for that matter adults—acquire progressively more complex physical and intellectual skills, as well as social skills and patterns of social (or unsocial) behavior.

SOCIALIZATION

Imitation helps account for much of a person's social behavior, not only in infancy and early childhood, but during the periods of adolescence and adulthood as well. At every state of development, we have a need for acceptance and approval. Conforming to the behavior patterns of others and acting in accordance with their social or moral standards is often a most effective, and sometimes the only, way of satisfying these needs.

The preschooler and, to a lesser extent, the elementary school child is almost completely dependent on her parents or some parent substitute for the satisfaction of her social needs. Early in life, the child discovers that she is rewarded for imitating certain behaviors of her parents and is perhaps punished for not imitating them in certain respects. When she first begins to use a spoon more or less as they do, to take a very simple example, they are likely to indicate their approval. If they do not, they should. They should neither expect nor wait for mastery before doing so but should register their approval of even slight progress toward or approximation of the desired behavior. When this is done, the child will very likely continue to try to act as they do, not only with respect to dining utensils but also in other situations where their praise is contingent upon her doing so.

Children do not always or necessarily imitate, or attempt to identify with, their parents. In some situations they might simply lack the ability or level of maturation necessary to do so. Sometimes they might not want to. Sometimes they may find that they are actually punished for imitating their parents for using foul language or drinking or smoking, for example. Sometimes they find it more rewarding to imitate others instead. Sometimes the child's attitude toward his parents is such that he deliberately or perhaps unconsciously tries to appear as different from them as possible, in which case they serve as so-called negative models. But ordinarily, the young child learns to do what his parents do, believe what they believe, like what they like, want what they want, and reject what they reject. In this way, the foundations of his value system, moral code, and system of social relationships are lain.

I know of no more effective way than the "good example" of teaching consideration for others, good citizenship, character, moral altruism, or love of one's fellow human beings. A child who regularly observes acts of kindness, courtesy, generosity, and sacrifice in his home is likely to act in the same way, especially if such behavior on his part is recognized and rewarded. A child, on the other hand, who is exposed to frequent lying or selfish or brutal behavior is likely to imitate that model. Here again, social or moral education is not only a matter of imitation. But when combined with reinforcement, it is likely to be far more effective than yelling, scolding, preaching, or threatening.

CONFORMITY

As the child approaches adolescence and becomes increasingly preoccupied with the recognition and approval of his peers, he can be expected to begin imitating them instead of, or in addition to, his parents. At this stage, of course, he might find it necessary, for the sake of his image or his status or his personal identity, to do what "everyone else" is doing, everyone else usually meaning a few people of his own age whose companionship he temporarily values. Since he is now likely to perceive being "different" as a situation to be avoided at practically any cost, we have the well-known phenomenon of teenagers slavishly imitating one another in such matters as speech, clothing and hair styles, tastes in music, dedication to "causes," attitudes toward social coventions, and moral codes.

31

Even into adulthood, a person might find it uncomfortable, if not downright dangerous, to behave too differently from his neighbors or to hold views at variance with theirs. He might learn, for example, that if he values his social standing in the neighborhood he simply cannot allow crabgrass to take over his lawn when everyone else on the block is practically paranoid about eradicating it. Nor is it safe for him to speak in defense of "those people" when most of his associates are denigrating them. So the patterns of conformity and imitation for the sake of social acceptance continue.

Conformity to the rules and regulations, the customs and conventions, of one's group is not, of course, always or necessarily bad. In fact, a certain kind and degree of conformity is what social living is all about. This is not the place to debate the pros and cons of conformity. But it is the place to note that throughout life not only a person's overt behavior but his attitudes and values, likes and dislikes, preferences and prejudices, his good and bad habits, his moral character, and his particular personality traits, and even the manner in which he expresses or attempts to express his individuality are very likely due, at least in part, to imitation or the closely related mechanism of identification.

IDENTIFICATION

While imitation is usually defined as the reproduction of particular, discrete behavior, there is no one precise meaning of the term *identification* as it is used in this context. Identification is commonly regarded as one of the so-called defense or psychological mechanisms that people use, often subconsciously, in order to protect their egos, enhance their self concepts, or to escape from what they perceive as threats to their emotional well-being. But just exactly how and why it works is not clear.

Somehow, by means of this mechanism, an individual not only attributes to himself, but actually assimilates the desirable characteristics of someone else. He internalizes the other person's attitudes, values, goals, beliefs, etc., and in a sense "becomes" that other person. Thus, he is able to perceive himself, or tries to have others perceive him, as similar to an individual whom he admires or is part of a group with which he would like to be associated. It would be difficult to exaggerate the importance of identification as a means of helping a person satisfy his social needs, particularly his need for affiliation, as well as an ego-building device that contributes significantly to his feeling of personal worth.

The child who tries to imitate an older brother or sister is identifying. So is the reader who puts herself in the shoes of the heroine of a novel she is reading. In still a different way identification is being used by the name-dropper who implies that he is personally acquainted with some celebrity or other, or that he is an accepted member of the "in" group. The individual who is ostentatiously proud of his race or nationality or club or political party, the student with a great deal of "school spirit," the tattler who tries to associate himself with the teacher against the forces of evil in the classroom—all of these are identifying, though not necessarily imitating.

While identification pertains to a broad, general, and sometimes subconscious attempt to be associated with others or to share their admired traits, imitation refers to the copying of specific ways of acting. A person could conceivably imitate for purposes other than identification, and he might attempt to identify without necessarily imitating. But quite often imitation and identification are likely to accompany one another.

IMITATION AND DELIBERATION

Imitative learning can be deliberate or automatic. Deliberate imitation is purposeful. It is motivated. It occurs when one person attentively observes another's behavior with the intention of thereafter trying to act in the same or a similar manner. The imitator acts consciously in order to achieve some goal or attain some end that he finds attractive. One example of deliberate imitative learning would be the Little Leaguer who watches the way his coach stands at the plate and holds his bat, and then tries to do the same.

Automatic imitation is unintentional. It occurs when a person "picks up" the mannerisms or behavior of another without realizing that he is doing so. This type of imitation serves no real purpose in the sense of contributing directly toward the individual's attainment of this goal, but it does nevertheless take place. If, for example, the baseball coach habitually tugs his cap before approaching the plate, our Little Leaguer might—perhaps inadvertently—come to act in like manner. If the Little Leaguer intentionally copies the cap-tugging behavior his imitation is, of course, of the deliberate variety.

It is not always possible to draw a sharp line between voluntary and involuntary, conscious and unconscious, or deliberate and automatic imitation. But we do sometimes assimilate the behaviors of others without setting out to do so, particularly if we admire the other person or have a need or desire to identify with him. Sometimes we imitate even against our will, or our better judgment. An individual who is constantly in the company of people who use coarse language, for example, might find himself imitating them even though he would rather not. ("Now you've got me saying it.") Sometimes it requires a special effort to avoid undesirable, indeliberate imitation.

Imitation is a two-way process. Not only do students imitate their teachers but teachers imitate their students. For identification purposes some high school and college teachers go out of their way, sometimes to ridiculous lengths, to imitate the speech patterns or clothing styles of their students. Or they end up habitually using such conversational gems as "like," "man," and "you know," even though they hate themselves for doing so.

MODELING

The teacher behavior that corresponds to imitative learning is called modeling. Like imitation itself, modeling can also be deliberate (formal) or unintentional (informal). When a father puts on a big show of eating his vegetables with what he tries to convey as the greatest of enjoyment, all for the benefit of his young son who is reluctant to approach them, he is modeling deliberately. If he burps and wipes his mouth on his sleeve after doing so, he is modeling—I hope—unintentionally. When a teacher explicitly says to his students: "Now watch how I do it, okay? Have you got it? Now you try it," he is modeling formally. But at the same time, he might be modeling other behavior informally.

Informal is far more common than formal modeling. Informal modeling is very likely going on in the classroom, as it is in the home, all the time. It occurs whenever the teacher is not consciously demonstrating a procedure or setting an example, but is nevertheless imitated whether she knows it or not. Much of what we referred to in Chapter 1 as incidental learning results from unintentional modeling.

Whenever a teacher is courteous, for example, or speaks gramatically, or dresses neatly, or conveys the impression that she considers the subject she is teaching to be interesting, exciting, and important, she is modeling a particular set of values. If, on the other hand, she is discourteous, speaks ungrammatically, dresses sloppily, or indicates without saying so explicitly that she regards her subject matter as dull or unimportant, she is modeling (or teaching) other values.

Teachers, like parents, cannot avoid being models. They really have no choice in the matter. The choice they do have is the kind of behavior they are going to model. Thus, a teacher should deliberately try to model friendly, honest behavior, fairness, good workmanship, and other qualities she would like her students to imitate even though they are not specified in her lesson plan; and she should be very careful not to model behavior which she would rather they did not imitate.

While formal, intentional modeling is the more efficient way of teaching most psychomotor as well as many academic skills, informal modeling is likely to be far more significant for social learning and the acquisition of values, ideals, attitudes, and other personality traits. Intentional modeling is itself a skill; its effectiveness depends upon what the teacher herself is able to do. Unintentional modeling is more a matter of the teacher's character and personality; its consequences are largely a function of the kind of person she is.

VARIETIES OF MODELS

Children and adolescents usually try to model themselves after older (but not much older) people of their own sex, particularly

35

if they are somehow rewarded with approval for doing so. In the first dozen years or so of life, since the child is so dependent upon his parents and teachers for the satisfaction of his social as well as certain other needs, they are likely to be his main models. But they are not, of course, his only models. Sometimes they are assisted by, and often they must compete with, other models.

A child might, and frequently does, identify with his friends or siblings, some popular entertainer or sports star, some fictional character from a movie or television show, some historical personage, or some famous statesman, humanitarian, or scientist. He might create an imaginary model to imitate—a kind of ideal self. But he might also choose to imitate the neighborhood punk or creep or ne'er-do-well. In short, just about anyone can serve as a model, but ordinarily individuals who are respected or admired, who are perceived as competent in a particular area, attractive, prestigious or powerful, are selected for that role.

One of the difficulties of being a parent or a teacher arises from the fact that through such media as television, movies, comic books, and magazines, children and young people are readily exposed to undesirable models who sometimes counteract or undo modeling in the home or school. Whether or to what extent the violence and brutality, the disrespect for authority, the sexual exploitation and perversions, the greed and materialism and callousness so common in our society can be attributed to certain media models remains a question to which there is no simple, clear-cut answer. But there is no reason at all to doubt that cruel, selfish, antisocial behavior, as well as the opposite kinds, are learned at least in part through imitation.

INDEPENDENT THINKING

Imitative learning, as we have seen, goes a long way toward explaining undesirable, as well as desirable, kinds of conformity. But what about nonconforming behavior? Creativity? Originality? Independent thinking? We certainly do not learn to think independently by simply replicating the thought patterns of others, nor is creativity simply a matter of copying models. But certain forms of behavior which contribute to, if they do not actually constitute, original thinking can be both modeled and imitated.

For example, good independent thinkers are intellectually honest. They have open minds and active curiosities. They gather information carefully and are precise in verifying it. They sift and evaluate data before acting on it. They suspend their judgment until enough data have been accumulated to warrant the drawing of a conclusion. They do not, in other words, jump to conclusions, nor do they pretend to have all of the answers. They seek out the views of others, listen to them carefully, respect them, and make an effort to understand them. Such behaviors can be modeled and might be imitated.

Good, original, independent thinkers have a detached love of truth, an appreciation of good thinking on the part of others, and a respect for evidence. They have enough humility to recognize their ignorance and admit their mistakes. They are more interested in solving problems or overcoming ignorance then they are in winning an argument or appearing to be brilliant. They maintain an appropriate balance between flexibility and decisiveness. They are willing and able to change their views when circumstances or new knowledge warrant their doing so. But they have the courage to maintain their convictions when they are as certain as possible that those convictions are worth maintaining. These kinds of behaviors also lend themselves to imitation.

Independent thinkers are sensitive to defects or shortcomings in the status quo. They recognize and are not afraid to point out the need for new and better ways of doing or expressing things. They have the courage to advance ideas that others might regard as unconventional, or even laugh at, but they do not deliberately go out of their way to imitate others who are unconventional, nor to fashion for themselves an image of unconventionality.

Authentic independent thinkers do a lot of other things, some of which we shall discuss in Chapters 5 and 6. In the present context of learning through imitation and teaching through modeling, I should like to suggest that instead of simply telling her students to do these kinds of things, the teacher should try to do them herself.

TRIAL AND ERROR

So far we have noted that a great deal of affective, as well as cognitive and psychomotor, learning results from the deliberate cognitive and psychomotor, learning results from the deliberate or automatic imitation of some model. But how does imitation itself take place? Imitation is not a pure, simple, fundamental form of learning. It is, rather, a process that embraces more elemental forms, particularly conditioning and trial and error. We shall discuss conditioning in the next chapter. First let's take a look at trial and error.

Trial and error learning is characteristic of the "self-made" or self-taught person, the one who has learned "the hard way," through "bitter experience" in the "school of hard knocks." But it is also a means by which all of us have learned many of the kinds of things mentioned earlier in this chapter in connection with imitation.

Trial and error learning can occur without imitation, but it is doubtful that imitative learning occurs without trial and error. A person might, for example, teach himself how to play the piano, through trial and error, without benefit of a model or any formal instruction. But if he does try to imitate a model, chances are that he will make a lot of mistakes before he attains a reasonable degree of proficiency.

Whether it's a case of learning to play a musical instrument, or to solve mathematical problems, or to eat with a knife and fork or with chopsticks, to speak a foreign language or read one's own language, or to be popular with the other sex, an element of imitation might well be present. But imitative learning is rarely a matter of simply and directly, much less perfectly, copying a model. More likely it involves repeated, sometimes awkward, often unsuccessful attempts, failure, and a feeling of frustration. It involves the recognition of one's mistakes and attempts to reduce or eliminate them. Ordinarily imitative learning involves an eventual degree of success, the refinement of one's productive efforts, and a gradual approximation of the desired behavior. Depending on the nature of the material or skill to be learned, all of this trial-and-erroring might take anywhere from a few moments to several years.

TRIAL AND SUCCESS

Actually we do not learn as much or as well by trial and error as we do by trial and success. The implication here is that we do not learn a successful way of behaving by acting unsuccessfully, but by repeatedly performing the successful behavior. This is not the hair-splitting distinction it might appear to be. As we shall see later, it is directly related to the principle of positive reinforcement and has important applications for a teacher who is guiding this type of learning. Despite the legitimate objection to the term trial and error, let's continue to refer to this kind of learning by that more familiar name.

Trial and error learning sometimes involves, or is at least very closely related to, learning by discovery, problem solving, inference, and creativity as well as imitation and conditioning. Like most other forms of learning, it presupposes motivation, includes retention and transfer, and is likely to be more effective with than without some form of teacher guidance. So do not expect this section alone to give you a complete analysis of trial and error—or trial and success—learning. In fact, no one section or chapter in and of itself will provide a complete overview of learning simply because the various forms of learning and the many factors that enter into any one of them are so closely interrelated. For purposes of analysis we can, however, examine how the trial and error aspect of learning works.

ACQUISITION OF SKILLS

Trial and error learning can perhaps best be illustrated with reference to psychomotor skills. In fact, it is hard to imagine a person acquiring any skill without it. Let's take swimming as an example. Whether or not he is deliberately trying to imitate a model, the beginning swimmer typically makes many random, clumsy, and often useless bodily motions in the initial stages of his learning. He wastes a great deal of energy kicking, splashing, and gasping for air, usually in a rather haphazard manner. Many of his trial motions, as he soon discovers, are of little or no avail. Some of them might actually be counter-productive.

Through his own experience he might gradually find that some of his movements are more beneficial than others. Consequently, he repeats those productive motions and abandons those that do not seem to be contributing to his progress. By continued practice, he is able to identify and subsequently avoid other errors. Perhaps quite by chance he "hits on" a rewarding movement which he then repeats and tries to perfect. Perhaps he does not just accidentally happen to hit on the successful motions. Perhaps he arrives at them through a process of logical reasoning, and "figures out" for himself a better way of proceeding. In any case, even without an instructor or a model to follow, through this trial and error procedure, he might learn to swim quite well. And then again he might not.

The old adage that practice makes perfect is not necessarily true. Practice alone, without guidance and feedback, could turn out to be nothing more than the repetition of one's mistakes, possibly to the point where they become so deeply ingrained that it is next to impossible to extinguish them. I doubt very much that I could improve my swimming or my French pronunciation or learn how to repair a television set, to take but a few of many possible examples, by means of undirected practice or independent trial and error. But on the other hand, I cannot even imagine myself learning such skills without trying, making mistakes, trying again, improving, and hopefully eventually succeeding.

TEACHER AND STUDENT ROLES

Strictly speaking, teachers are not absolutely necessary for trial and error learning. It can and often does take place without them. Theoretically, if a person lived long enough and wanted to badly enough, he could learn just about anything he would need to know through his own efforts. But such unguided learning would hardly be economical or generally feasible—which is why we have schools.

Trial and error learning is unquestionably most efficient when it is accompanied by systematic instruction. The role of an instructor in facilitating such learning is to provide a suitable model, to point out faults and make suggestions for overcoming them. She demonstrates or explains how the learner can improve. She keeps him informed of his progress, offers encouragement and support, and reinforces "successive approximations" of the desired behavior. Finally, the instructor helps the learner integrate and coordinate the various sub-skills (or "parts") that go to make up the "whole" complex behavior.

Successful trial and error learning also depends on certain qualities of the learner. He needs, among other things, a strong desire to learn the new behavior and enough determination to persevere, particularly when the going gets tough and he does not seem to be making much progress. He also needs to have attained the appropriate level of physical maturation or intellectual development and the necessary degree of competence in the simpler skills required for those which are more complex.

While practice alone, as has been suggested, will not make him perfect, it is inconceivable that a learner will approach perfection without it. Therefore, he needs incentives to practice, opportunities to try, freedom to make mistakes and fail, and a chance to profit from his mistakes. Mistakes are sometimes painful. But this is part of the price of learning certain kinds of behavior which cannot really be learned in any other way.

PROBLEM SOLVING

Trial and error enters into forms of learning other than the acquisition of psychomotor skills. It helps explain some of our affective and cognitive learning as well, and it certainly plays an important part in the process of problem solving.

As we shall see in Chapter 5, the very heart of the problem solving process is the formulation and verification (or trying out) of hypotheses. An hypothesis is a hunch or a kind of educated guess as to what should be done in a given situation; it is a tentative solution to a problem based on available but incomplete information. Hypotheses are usually stated, at least implicitly, in if–then terms: *If* we do this, *then* that will probably follow. If we do the other thing, then something else is likely to occur. This, of course, is what scientific research is often all about: to find out whether such-and-such will indeed lead to so-and-so.

When confronted with a novel situation that we are not sure how to deal with, our first response usually is to draw on our memory and try to recall what we did in similar previous situations.

We are also likely to observe others to see what they have done or are doing in the same or a similar situation. Largely on the basis of memory and observation, we formulate hypotheses. But if we are wise, we "try out" a number of possible strategies instead of acting precipitously on the first hypothesis or course of action that comes to mind.

In some situations circumstances are such that we simply cannot try out all of our hypotheses overtly, so we test them mentally or symbolically instead. We attempt, in other words, to foresee the probable consequences of alternative courses of action that are open to us. Thus, we reject some possibilities, perhaps modify or combine others, and eventually narrow the field down to the one strategy that appears to be most promising.

Let's take a rather common type of example. Here is Becki, a normal, healthy, 15-year-old girl, new in the neighborhood, new in her school. (Becki, incidentally, did not learn to spell her name as she does through trial and error. It just so happens that among her classmates are girls who sign their names Debbi, Kathi, Sandi, and Mari.) Naturally, she wants to make friends in her new school, but she is not sure how to proceed. She observes that Lynn is very popular with the other girls as well as the boys in her class.

"Maybe," Becki reasons, "I should try to be like Lynn. But Yolanda is also very popular—and she's so different from Lynn. Maybe I ought to imitate Yolanda instead. Or maybe I could try imitating Lynn for a few days and then if that doesn't work, I can imitate Yolanda for a while. But what specifically is it about Lynn that makes her so attractive? I can't very well copy everything she does because, after all, she's Lynn and I'm me, Becki.

"Maybe if I just wore my hair the way Yolanda does, or dressed more like Lynn. But let's face it, Yolanda's hair wouldn't go with my face and on me Lynn's clothes would look like. . .

"Maybe if I could learn to smile the way they do. Maybe I should just smile my own smile more often. Maybe if I just went and sat down with them some day. But then they might think I'm too pushy. . .

"Maybe if I'd go off by myself every day so they'd see how lonely I am. . .but then they might think I'm weird or snobbish. . .

"Maybe if I invited them to a party. . .But then they might think I'm just trying to buy their friendship. . .

"Maybe I ought not to be so much of a 'brain' in class. . .
"Maybe if I did this. . .Maybe if I did that. . ."

SYMBOLIC TRIAL AND ERROR

In trying to solve what for her is a genuine and tremendously important problem, Becki is learning by means of symbolic trial and error. In so doing, she is thinking. She is employing essentially the same procedure that statesmen, scientists, economists, businessmen, military strategists, and teachers, among others, employ in trying to solve their problems, and that you and I might use in trying to solve ours.

Even in solving relatively simple everyday problems, to say nothing of loftier matters such as putting together one's philosophy of life, the thinking process rarely proceeds in a neat, orderly sequence with one idea (or symbol) directly leading to the next and so on to a conclusion. The process, rather, is typically disorderly, mixed up, and characterized by sometimes wild guesses, false starts, back-tracking, the discarding of some ideas and the assimilation of others. Ordinarily it includes distractions and digressions, temporary feelings of futility and discouragement, periods of dormancy during which nothing much seems to be happening. Eventually, if we are lucky or if we persevere long enough, the parts fall into place, patterns of relationships begin to form, and there emerges—sometimes quite suddenly—the solution or conclusion we have been seeking.

But now we are getting ahead of our story. Let's postpone until later chapters further discussion of problem solving and other forms of thinking. For the present, let's simply try to recognize why and how these "higher mental processes" include a particular kind of trial and error activity.

SUMMARY

Some of our most important learning is imitative. It is largely, though not entirely, through imitation, for example, that we learn language, on which so much of our subsequent learning—through listening and reading—depends. Many of our psychomotor, cognitive, and social skills, as well as patterns of social or unsocial behavior are also learned through the observation and imitation of others. Certain forms of behavior which contribute to, if they do not actually constitute, independent thinking can also be acquired in this way.

Imitative learning is sometimes deliberate, sometimes unintentional and possibly unconscious. The same is true of modeling. Teachers, like parents, are constantly modeling whether or not they are consciously aware of doing so. They cannot avoid being models. They really have no choice in the matter. They do, however, have a choice as to the kinds of behavior they will model.

As children mature, they tend to identify with people other than their parents and teachers, especially with individuals or groups whom they admire or perceive as powerful or somehow attractive. One of the difficulties of being a parent or a teacher arises from the fact that children and young people are easily exposed to, and sometimes victimized by, undesirable models who counteract the good examples given in the home or school.

Imitation is not a pure and simple form of learning. Rather, it embraces other forms of learning, such as conditioning and trial and error. Trial and error learning, in turn, overlaps with discovery, inference, creativity, and other ways of thinking and learning that are discussed in the chapters ahead. All of these are so closely interrelated that in practice it is sometimes impossible to separate one from the other. Problem solving, for example, can be thought of as a kind of symbolic trial and error process.

Actually, we do not learn by trial and error so much as we do by trial and success. But avoiding mistakes is certainly a part of the process. This form of learning requires practice, but without guidance and direction, feedback and reinforcement, practice alone is likely to be of little avail. Thus, trial and error learning is likely to be most effective when accompanied by systematic instruction, including modeling.

Recommended Readings

Bandura, Albert. "Analysis of Modeling Processes " in Albert Bandura, ed., *Psychological Modeling.* New York: Lieber-Atherton, 1974. A very good overview of modeling by one of the foremost authorities on the subject. Summarizes research and discusses various issues and interpretations from the standpoint of social learning.

Bany, Mary A., and Johnson, Lois V. *Educational Social Psychology.* New York: Macmillan, 1975. Includes a readable discussion of such topics as the process of conformity, language and communication, group influences on motivation and achievement, and the learning of attitudes.

Brown, Roger. "The Role of Imitation (or Learning by Identification) in Moral Conduct" in M.D. Gall and B.A. Ward, eds., *Critical Issues in Educational Psychology.* Boston: Little, Brown, 1974. In this short excerpt from his book *Social Psychology* (New York: Free Press, 1965) the author shows the relationship between modeling and reinforcement in moral eduction.

Chomsky, Noam. *Language and Mind.* New York: Harcourt, Brace, Jovanovich, 1972. By no means easy reading, but well worth the effort on the part of anyone seriously interested in psycholinguistics. The author and his views are mentioned in this chapter, but very briefly.

Miller, Neal E., and Dollard, John. *Social Learning and Imitation.* New Haven: Yale University Press, 1941. Old enough and still widely enough read to be considered a classic in its field.

Slobin, Daniel I. "Imitation and Grammatical Development in Children" in Bandura, *Psychological Modeling,* mentioned above. A short article (about 10 pages) that does justice to the subject specified in its title.

Stephens, Thomas M. "Using Reinforcement and Social Modeling with Delinquent Youth." *Review of Educational Research,* Summer, 1973. A comprehensive review of research on the subject. A good source of more detailed information.

Surgeon General's Scientific Advisory Committee on Television and Social Behavior. *Television and Growing Up: The Impact of Televised Violence.* Washington: U.S. Government Printing Office, 1972. Discusses the impact of home and family as well as television and other factors on aggressive behavior. Does not clearly blame or absolve television.

3

Learning through Conditioning

Both imitative and trial and error learning, as we have seen, often involve some form of conditioning. It has, in fact, been argued that conditioning necessarily enters into each of them. Some types of learning require little if any trial and error or imitation. For that matter, they require little or no thinking or even understanding. Such learning can also be explained in terms of conditioning. In short, just about any of the kinds and ways of learning that we have discussed or will discuss in later chapters can be construed as necessarily including at least an element of conditioning.

You will, I hope, recall our brief reference to conditioning in Chapter 1. We noted there that conditioning is basic to association theories of learning. In this chapter we shall explore the concept of conditioning in more detail. To begin with, we should recognize a distinction between two forms of conditioning: classical and operant. Of the two, the latter has the more widespread applicability. We shall consider operant conditioning later in this chapter, but first let's take a look at classical conditioning.

CLASSICAL CONDITIONING

Classical conditioning is essentially the pairing (or the substitution) of stimuli so as to form particular associations. Its prototype is the experimental work of Ivan Pavlov on the conditioned response. Some contemporary behavioral psychologists see all learning—indeed all human behavior—as a set of conditioned responses. Some have refined Pavlov's principles extensively and in so doing have contributed to the development of the more sophisticated concept of operant conditioning.

One need not be a confirmed behaviorist to recognize that some forms of learning involve nothing more than the simple association of one idea or experience with another. Many of us, for example, have already been conditioned to associate the name Pavlov with the image of a salivating dog. We might also have been conditioned to accept or reject Pavlovian principles as adequate explanations of some (or all) of our own behavior. Some of us may have been conditioned to react negatively to the very word "conditioning."

Classical conditioning is sometimes referred to as Pavlovian conditioning, or simple conditioning, or respondent conditioning. By the time you finish reading this paragraph, if you are reading attentively, you will probably have been conditoned to associate classical with respondent conditioning and either or both with friend Pavlov. But maybe you are a bit hazy about Pavlov, so let's briefly review his major contributions to our understanding of how certain kinds of learning take place.

PAVLOV AND HIS DOG

Ivan Pavlov was a Russian physiologist—note that he did not regard himself as a psychologist—who was awarded the Nobel prize for medicine in 1904. In connection with his research on

48

the digestive process in animals, he observed that as he approached one of his laboratory dogs with food (meat powder), the dog began to salivate. This was hardly a surprise. The stimulus food naturally elicited the response salivation. In the parlance of behavioral psychology, both the stimulus and the response were "unconditioned."

As part of the experiment a bell was sounded a second or so before the food was presented. When this was done, the dog salivated—not, at first, in response to the bell, but to the food. After a dozen or so trials, the auditory stimulus was presented, but the food was withheld. The dog, nevertheless, responded in the same way. It had "learned" to drool in response to the sound as it had originally responded to the sight or smell of the food. The dog's reaction to the bell has even since been regarded as the classic example of a conditioned response.

Though Pavlov's discovery of the conditioned response resulted from research with animals, the principle was applied to human learning as well and remains one of the cornerstones of contemporary association, stimulus-response, or behavioral theories of learning. Simply stated the principle is this: when a stimulus that is neutral with respect to a particular response is frequently associated with a stimulus that elicits that response, the originally neutral stimulus will itself come to elicit the same response.

Subsequent research in Pavlov's laboratory showed that after a conditioned response had been produced, the conditioned (originally ineffective) stimulus could be used as an unconditioned (adequate) stimulus in producing new conditioned responses. For example, after a dog had learned to salivate in response to an auditory stimulus (a metronome) without the presence of food, the metronome was sounded at the same time that the dog was shown a visual stimulus (a black square.) After a number of such paired exposures, the black square came to elicit the same salivary response that first the food and later the metronome had produced. Presumably, the dog could have been conditioned to salivate next in response to a green square, to the word green, to the spoken command "Drool!" and so forth.

Pavlov and his associates found that when the conditioned stimulus (the bell) was presented a number of times without the unconditioned stimulus (the food), the amount of saliva that dropped from the dog's mouth began to decrease until after a dozen or so trials there was none at all. The conditioned response, in technical terms, had been extinguished. They also found that a dog could be conditioned to generalize and discriminate, that is, to respond in the same way to a variety of stimuli which were similar to one another and to distinguish between those which were different from each other.

These basic Pavlovian principles explain why any dog might drool or act excited at the sound of a can opener opening a can of dog food. They explain how he learns to respond differentially to various kinds of foods or sounds or voices or other stimuli. They suggest a method of teaching dogs and other animals to perform tricks or to carry out specified orders. But what about human learning? Classical conditoning helps explain why, for example, a person might respond to the word *steak* somewhat as he would to an actual tender, juicy, mouth-watering, medium rare sirloin. But as John B. Watson demonstrated, the principles have other more important and far-reaching applications than that.

WATSON AND HIS RAT

In the early 1920s, John Watson, an American psychologist, began applying Pavlovian principles to human emotional learning. Watson, who is acknowledged to be the "father" or founder of behavioristic psychology, is best remembered for his famous experiment in which he conditioned an eleven-month-old boy named Albert to fear a rat. You might be wondering why anyone would deliberately try to frighten an eleven-month-old infant with a rat, but stranger things than that have been done in the name of science.

When first given the rat to play with, Albert's reaction was neutral. He gave no indication of fear whatsoever. But Watson had previously observed that children of Albert's age did appear to be frightened by loud, sudden noises. These symptoms of fright were unlearned, involuntary reflex responses. As part of his experiment, Watson struck a hammer against a piece of metal just as Albert was about to touch the rat. After this procedure was repeated a number of times, Albert came to respond to the rat alone as he had previously responded—by whimpering—to the loud noise.

Having demonstrated the possibility and methodology of "teaching" a child to fear a rat, Watson reasoned that it was possible, using essentially the same procedure, to condition a child to fear anything else. By the same token, if a child could be conditoned to fear anything, he could be conditioned to hate or reject or approach or do just about anything that Watson wanted him to do. This line of reasoning led Watson to make the claim (previously made by many others, incidentally) that if he were given a free hand in "educating" a young child, he could make of that person just about anything he wished.

Watson never even tried to make good his claim, but some contemporary "behavioral engineers" have by no means abandoned that possibility. In the meantime, parents, teachers, politicians, advertisers, propagandists, and clergymen, among others, who might never have heard of Watson have been using, in some cases quite successfully, the techniques that he and Pavlov made famous. Thus, whether we like it or not, some of the things you and I have learned were learned in essentially the same way that Pavlov's dog learned to salivate in response to a buzzer and little Albert learned to recoil from white rats.

CLASSICAL CONDITIONING AS USED BY
PAVLOV AND WATSON

Unconditioned Stimulus (US) ──────────→	Unconditioned Response (UR)
US + CS ──────────→ UR	
Conditioned Stimulus (CS) ──────────→	Conditioned Response (CR)

Meat (US) ──────────→	Flow of saliva (UR)
Bell (CS) at first ──────────→	No flow of saliva
Meat + Bell ──────────→	Flow of saliva (UR)
Bell (CS) without meat ──────────→	Flow of saliva (CR)

Noise (US) ──────────→	Whimpering (UR)
Rat (CS) at first ──────────→	No whimpering
Noise + Rat ──────────→	Whimpering (UR)
Rat (CS) without noise ──────────→	Whimpering (CR)

EMOTIONAL LEARNING

Classical conditioning does seem to account for much of our affective or emotionally-toned learning: our likes and dislikes, our fears and anxieties, etc. We might, for example, like or dislike a particular song, not so much because of any quality in the song itself, but because of certain pleasant or unpleasant experiences with which we associate it.

Similarly, our positive or negative attitudes toward certain people, or kinds or classes of people, might also have been acquired principally by means of conditioned associations. We might, for example, have been deliberately taught to associate X type people with goodness and type Y people with badness. Or we might have formed these associations largely on the basis of our own (usually very limited) experience. But in any case, we might respond to the sight or even the name of type Y people much as we would to some more fundamental stimulus that implies badness or avoidance.

It is through the process of classical conditioning that certain objects or situations, such as a picture of a snake or even the word snake, which in and of themselves are quite harmless, might elicit in us a feeling of intense discomfort. Please note that the picture or the word is a conditioned stimulus, a substitute for the snake itself. Note also that a person's fear of real snakes is itself a conditioned response.

Withdrawal from or trepidation at the sight of a snake is an acquired response, learned very likely through imitation. But if we scream at or run away from a snake that we know to be harmless, our behavior—even though it is imitative—is still a good example of a conditioned response. It is not so much the snake itself which causes us to act as we do, but our recollections of other people fleeing from (or picking up and handling) snakes.

Just as many of our fears are learned through conditioning, so can they be overcome or at least alleviated by counterconditioning or desensitization. Counterconditioning is the process of conditioning a person to behave in a manner that is incompatible with the behavior one is attempting to extinguish. Desensitization is the process of weakening a person's fear of or anxiety about some object or situation by gradually increasing his exposure to and tolerance of the thing feared. A snake, for example, can be first presented at a distance and then gradually brought closer and closer while the fearful person is otherwise comfortable, relaxed and doing something enjoyable. A variation of this procedure is to have the fearful person begin by simply imagining himself very slowly approaching a snake.

One of Watson's disciples, after having conditioned a child to fear a rabbit, counterconditioned him not only to tolerate but actually pat the rabbit. In this experiment, instead of having a loud, sudden noise accompanying the rabbit, the child was given some candy as the rabbit was brought nearer and nearer. Similar methods, based on the same principle, have been used with varying degrees of success in helping people learn to overcome a variety of fears and phobias. They are also used by people whose job it is to "make" us want or reject what they want us to.

VERBAL ASSOCIATIONS

Classical conditioning helps explain some of our simpler cognitive learning, particularly that involving verbal associations. Consider again the acquisition of language, which was described in the previous chapter as largely a matter of imitation. I suspect that it was largely through imitation that you first pronounced the word *candy*, for example. But as a very young child, you were probably conditioned to respond to the spoken word *candy* much as you did to the candy itself. Maybe you did not exactly drool at the sound of the word, but you probably reached forward with your hands open or otherwise indicated that you would like some. Through conditioning you learned to associate the word with the thing and began to derive an understanding of what the word means.

Later in life, you might have been conditioned to respond to the printed word *candy* (or *steak* on a menu) much as you would to that spoken word. There is, as we have noted, a lot more to learning vocabulary and reading than imitation plus simple respondent conditioning. But here we have a clue as to how a person comes to associate written symbols with spoken words, and spoken words with corresponding objects.

Most of us have been conditioned to respond to traffic

signals as we would to a spoken directive from a police officer to "stop" or "go" or "slow down." Similarly, we respond to a particular slogan as some advertiser would have us respond, by thinking of (or imagining or remembering and maybe even buying) the product with which it has been so frequently and closely associated. Very likely, we have been so conditioned that whenever we see a picture of a portly, smiling, ho-ho-hoing senior citizen with a flowing snow-white beard and a white-trimmed suit of red, we cannot help—repeat: literally cannot help—thinking of other situations or events that we have been conditioned to refer to collectively as Christmas.

We may have been conditioned to associate 1776 so closely with the Declaration of Independence that we cannot help recalling the one whenever we encounter the other. We have probably been conditioned to associate Paris with France, Hamlet with Shakespeare, 9×7 with 63, muchacho with boy, H_2O with water, Lincoln with Gettysburg, etc.

Of course, we might not have the slightest idea of what H_2O means, or why or how it is related to water. We might not understand the significance of Gettysburg or what Hamlet is all about. But let's take one thing at a time. We shall get to the problem of meaning and understanding in the next chapter. For the present, let us simply note that some of our academic learning, particularly the type involving simple verbal associations and automatic responses, can be explained in terms of simple classical conditioning.

Previously learned simple associations help us make new and more complex associations. These previously learned associations are used as so-called mediating links and are essential to the process known as chaining. The chaining or linking of a number of associations so as to form an intricate network of associations is one way—not the only way, and not necessarily the best way—of explaining our higher mental processes, including understanding, problem-solving, and even creativity.

OPERANT CONDITIONING

Operant conditioning is most closely associated with B.F. Skinner, whose entire psychological system is based on that concept. Skinner has certainly done more than any other individual to popularize the concept. In so doing he has antagonized if not frightened a great many people with what has been interpreted as his denial of human freedom and dignity, and his suggestion that the future of civilization as we know it depends upon the manipulation of human beings and systematic control over their behavior by means of operant conditioning techniques which are commonly referred to as programming. One need not, of course, accept Skinner's philosophical assumptions about human nature in order to recognize that a great part of our learning is the result of operant conditioning.

Skinner and his disciples maintain that all learning can be accounted for in terms of operant (also known as instrumental) conditioning. I believe that, when combined with imitation, trial and error, or classical conditioning, it does account for very much though not all of our learned behavior, particularly that which is formally and deliberately taught. I would venture, therefore, that of the various ways of learning that we have thus far considered, operant conditioning has the most widespread applicability and is the most closely related to the work of a teacher.

VOLUNTARY BEHAVIOR

Classical conditioning explains many of the automatic, involuntary responses we have learned to make. It explains, for example, why I cannot help thinking of Abraham Lincoln whenever I hear of Gettysburg. The association has been practically forced upon me. Operant conditioning is more useful in explaining our voluntary behavior. I read about the Civil War, or speak favorably of Abraham Lincoln, or recite or listen attentively to someone else reciting the Gettysburg address, or I actually visit (or hope to visit) Gettysburg because I am or expect to be somehow rewarded for doing so, or because I have been rewarded for those or similar behaviors in the past. The actual, remembered or anticipated reward explains not only why I do the things I do, but how I learned to do them.

The word *operant* refers to any behavior that operates on

the environment in order to bring about reinforcement. It signifies a person's voluntary behavior as opposed to his simple reflex acts. Thus, anything that a person does intentionally—writing his name, reading a book, spelling the word *psychology,* playing the piano, writing or saying or thinking 2 + 2 + 2 = 6—might be an operant. According to the basic principles of operant conditioning, two and only two conditions are necessary for learning to occur: first, the response must be made (or the act or operant or behavior, whatever you wish to call it, be performed); second, it must be followed (usually the sooner the better) by positive reinforcement. Classical conditioning explains how or why we come to make a particular response in the first place. Operant conditioning helps explain why we continue to make it.

DESIRED AND UNDESIRED BEHAVIOR

Many of the things you have learned, whether in the cognitive, affective or psychomotor domain, are the result of systematic, deliberate instruction. Your teacher, whether it was a professional school teacher or your parents or perhaps an advertiser or newspaper columnist acting as a teacher, was attempting to change your behavior in some way or other. Teaching of any kind, as a matter of fact, is commonly thought of as essentially an attempt at behavior modification.

With respect to the concept of instruction as an attempt at changing or modifying students' behavior, a useful distinction can be made between two main kinds of such behavior. First, there are the "desired responses" which the teacher wants to produce or strengthen or maintain. These are the outcomes or the products that the student is expected to acquire. The advertiser wants you to buy his product. A mother wants her daughter to keep her room clean. A school teacher wants her pupils to be able to read, write, and add, to love their neighbors, to appreciate good poetry, to understand operant conditioning, etc. All of these are examples of what we are calling desired responses. They do not necessarily refer to your desires; they do refer to the desires of your teacher.

Secondly, there are "undesired responses" which the teacher wishes to eliminate or at least reduce. These are sometimes referred to as "deviant" or interfering" behaviors because they preclude or inhibit the learning of desired behaviors. This category includes all sorts of errors or misunderstandings, unsocial conduct, bad habits, unhealthy attitudes, behavior that might be injurious to oneself or others, etc. With respect to instruction, in short, undesired behaviors are those things which your teachers would rather you did not do.

The basic principle of operant conditioning is that you learned to make desired responses because you were somehow rewarded for doing so, and that you learned to avoid undesired responses because you were either not rewarded or because you were punished for making them.

THE LAW OF EFFECT

Operant conditioning is based not only on classical conditioning, but to a much greater extent on the law of effect, formulated in the early part of the twentieth century by Edward L. Thorndike. The author of some of the first and most influential books on the subject and one of the first professors to offer a university course in the area, Thorndike is generally regarded as the "father" of educational psychology. Among the most significant of his many contributions to the fields of educational psychology in general and learning theory in particular is his law of effect.

According to the law of effect, any behavior which has pleasant consequences is likely to be repeated and thus learned, while acts followed by unpleasant consequences are likely to be avoided and thus not learned or unlearned or extinguished. Thorndike offered other "laws" of learning, notably the law of exercise and the law of readiness. The law of exercise is the psychological justification of drill, repetition, review, or practice. The law of readiness suggests the need for preparing the individual for the learning experience. As a result of his experimentation, Thorndike observed that repetitive drill alone does not facilitate learning, a point that we noted in our discussion of trial and error learning. Consequently, he came to place greater emphasis on the law of effect, considering repetition as simply a means of providing conditions under which the law of effect can operate.

The law of effect explains the utility—indeed the necessity—of incentives, feedback, or some system of reward as indispensable conditions of learning. It underlies the basic principle of behavior modification that behavior is shaped by, if not determined by, its consequences. A corollary of the law of effect is that pleasant consequences are likely to be far more instrumental than unpleasant consequences in fostering new learned behavior.

POSITIVE REINFORCEMENT

Reinforcement is the key concept of operant conditioning and the one which distinguishes it most clearly from classical conditioning. The term positive reinforcement refers to any consequence or effect of a particular act that increases the probability of that act's recurring. The term implies some sort of reward.

In classical conditioning, the consequences of an act are irrelevant as far as the learning of that act is concerned. Reinforcement is superfluous. Pavlov did not "reward" his dog for salivating. He did not have to. Repeated presentation of the conditioned and unconditioned stimuli simultaneously was enough to bring about that conditioned response. Watson did not praise little Albert for cowering at the sight of a rat or give him an A on his report card for acting as he did. Nobody rewards me for thinking about baseball when I hear the Star Spangled Banner being played. But I think of it just the same.

In learning that occurs through classical conditioning, the stimuli that elicit the behavior are all that really matter. These, by the way, are called discriminative stimuli. One discriminative stimulus makes me do this; another that; a third, something else, etc., regardless of the consequences. In operant conditioning, the consequences of the act are critical. Far more compelling than the discriminative stimulus which precedes the response is the so-called reinforcing stimulus that follows it.

Here is how reinforcement is supposed to work. You did something once for the first time in your life. It does not matter why. But you used the word *please*, for example, or you said that Columbus discovered America, or you wrote 7 X 6 = 42, or you smiled at a person or went to a baseball game. Maybe you did so because of imitation. Maybe it was through trial and error. Maybe it was a classically-conditioned response. It does not matter. What does matter is that the consequences were somehow pleasant or rewarding, so you did it again. Again your behavior was positively reinforced, and so on until eventually that particular way of acting became habitual. In this way, you might very well have acquired the psychomotor and intellectual skills you possess, your language ability, your attitudes, values, beliefs, interests, your existing store of knowledge, and anything else you may have learned.

VARIETIES OF REINFORCERS

In the first chapter we noted that most human behavior is learned. It has just been suggested that one of the most crucial elements in most (if not all) forms of learning is reinforcement. This means that most of the things a person does—or knows or thinks or feels or believes—is somehow presently rewarding, or has been gratifying in the past, or is less dissatisfying than alternative behaviors would be.

The exact nature of the particular reinforcer in a given situation is not always apparent. But among the more common of them

$$S^D \longrightarrow R \longrightarrow S^R$$

OPERANT CONDITIONING MODEL (The Reinforcing Stimulus Is Contingent Upon The Student's Making The Desired Response)

Discriminative Stimulus	Response	Reinforcing Stimulus
The printed word *house*	Child says, *house*	Teacher says, *that's right!*
Teacher asks, *who wrote Hamlet?*	Student says, *Shakespeare*	Teacher smiles and nods her head in approval.

59

are food, money and the things that money will buy, a gesture of approval or a word of commendation from one's parents or teachers or friends or employer, some form of attention or recognition, the reduction or elimination of tensions or anxiety, a feeling of strength or power or importance, a "warm inner glow," etc. In a scholastic setting positive reinforcers are also likely to take the form of high quiz grades, good report card marks, a place on the honor roll or dean's list and that sort of thing.

A useful distinction can be made between what are called primary and secondary reinforcers. Primary or unconditioned reinforcers are such stimuli as food and drink, which are essential to the very maintenance of life. The reinforcing power of these physiological stimuli is natural rather than learned. Most reinforcers, however, are of the secondary or conditioned variety. These acquire their reinforcing power by having been associated with and substituted for primary reinforcers. Thus, the smile of a mother as she feeds her child, for example, might become a secondary reinforcer. Through the classical conditioning procedure, a spoken word can be substituted for the smile, a gesture or an object for the word, etc. Theoretically, just about anything of value to the individual can become a secondary reinforcer.

Certain stimuli which have been paired with a number of primary or secondary reinforcers acquire a general reinforcing effect. Money is one example of such a so-called generalized reinforcer. Attention, approval, and affection, which are commonly referred to as social reinforcers, are other examples. Certain objects, such as trophies, medals, certificates, and report card marks, are classed as symbolic reinforcers. Certain activities, such as playing a favorite game or watching television, are called activity reinforcers. So a broad variety of objects and situations are, or can become, positively reinforcing.

One of the most important functions of a teacher is to provide suitable and timely reinforcement—the most effective kind at the most auspicious moment in just the right amount. One difficulty with this function arises from the fact that what is reinforcing to one person is not always or necessarily or to the same degree reinforcing to another. The reinforcement function can be facilitated, however, by the fact that a student can (and should) learn to reinforce himself, automatically and from within, so that he is not constantly or completely dependent upon the teacher for some sort of extrinsic (external) reward.

NEGATIVE REINFORCEMENT

Some changes in behavior are due not so much to positive as they are to negative reinforcement. Let's see how negative reinforcement is related to positive reinforcement on the one hand, and to punishment on the other.

Earlier in this chapter we noted that teaching in the sense of conditioning is essentially a matter of eliciting "desired responses" on the part of the student and of reducing or eliminating "undesired responses." According to the principles of operant conditioning, there are three basic ways in which such behavioral changes can be produced; through positive reinforcement, negative reinforcement, or through the use of punishment.

Positive reinforcement, as we have seen, pertains to any object or event or situation that increases the probability of a person's doing something voluntarily, or of making a response that someone else desires, so as to be "rewarded" by pleasant consequences.

Negative reinforcement also pertains to any object or event or situation that increases the probability of a person's doing something voluntarily or of making a response that someone else desires. But in this case, the person acts as he does in order to avoid unpleasant consequences, or to terminate what psychologists call aversive (or noxious) stimuli.

Negative reinforcement occurs when doing a certain thing is followed by the avoidance of something that the individual finds unpleasant or the termination of a noxious situation. The release or escape from the aversive situation constitutes the reinforcement. For example, a person goes into an air conditioned theatre on a hot afternoon to escape the noxious heat of the sun. Maybe the particular movie that is being shown does not "turn him on" but the heat "turns him off." Being turned on corresponds roughly to positive reinforcement; avoiding a situation that turns one off, to negative reinforcement.

Negative reinforcement, along with punishment or the threat of punishment, is sometimes referred to as aversive control.

It accounts for the fact that we often do things mainly in order to avoid the consequences of not doing them. It is something like choosing the lesser of two evils—or of two aversive stimuli.

A person might learn to observe traffic regulations, for example, not because he is positively reinforced for obeying them, but to avoid having to pay a fine for violating them. She might work at her job for eight hours a day, even though she finds it unpleasant, in order to avoid the even less pleasant consequences of being out of work and having no money. A child might learn to brush her teeth in order to get her mother "off her back." Release from the aversive stimulus of her mother's "bugging" constitutes her reinforcement. A college student might study psychology to avoid the unpleasantness of flunking a test, failing the course, etc.

PUNISHMENT

As used in behavioral psychology, the term *punishment* does not have quite the same meaning that it does in ordinary usage. It does not, for example, carry with it any connotation of retribution or retaliation. It does, however, suggest a way of changing or "correcting" deviant or undesired behavior.

The line between negative reinforcement and punishment is rather fine. The first increases the probability of a response being made. The second decreases the probability. Both imply the avoidance of aversive stimuli. But negative reinforcement refers to a person's doing something in order to avoid them, while punishment applies to cases in which he does *not* behave in a certain way (or learns to refrain from making undesired responses) so as to avoid unpleasant consequences. These unpleasant consequences ordinarily take some form of physical or psychological pain (the presence of aversive stimuli) or deprivation (the withdrawal or withholding of a positive reinforcer).

Let's see how punishment works in everyday life. Suppose that some morning you decide that from now on you are going to be especially friendly and cheerful. You resolve to greet everyone you meet with a pleasant "Good morning" or "How Ya Doing?" If your friendly greeting is regularly returned, there is a high degree of probability that you will continue to act in that way.

But suppose that the people you greet look at you as though you were weird, or that they tell you to go to hell, or call the police. Chances are that you will not continue with your resolution much longer.

Let's take another situation as an example. Suppose that a child responds to a teacher's question by stating that Rome is the capital of England. Suppose further that he is consequently slapped, called stupid, kept after school, or otherwise made to experience some form of pain or deprivation. The expectation and the probability is that, in order to avoid similar aversive stimuli in the future, he will not make that particular mistake again. The next time he is asked, he might say that Paris or Canterbury or Timbuktu is the capital of England. There are, in fact, an infinite number of wrong answers he could give. So far, through punishment, he has not learned to make the desired response. He has only learned not to make that one particular undesired response.

If—through trial and error, through imitation of his teacher, through a form of classical conditioning, or in some other way— the student learns to give the correct answer, in order to avoid unpleasant consequences, the principle of negative reinforcement is operative. If, however, he responds in the desired manner because he has been, or expects to be, somehow rewarded for doing so, the principle of positive reinforcement is at work.

These distinctions might appear to be highly theoretical, and perhaps they are. In concrete situations, positive reinforcement, negative reinforcement, and punishment might all be involved. In comparing them, however, we should note that positive reinforcement is the most effective of these three means of promoting learning, punishment the least effective, and negative reinforcement somewhere in between.

EXTINCTION

As we noted in our discussion of classical conditioning, once an association between a conditioned stimulus and response is established, it does not necessarily remain permanent. So long as Pavlov's dog received food shortly after salivating in response to the buzzer, it continued to do so. But after a while when the

63

sounding of the buzzer was not followed by the food, the conditioned response was extinguished. In terms of classical conditioning, extinction occurs when the conditioned stimulus is presented without the unconditioned stimulus. In terms of operant conditioning, it occurs when reinforcement does not follow the response.

Consider, for example, a child who misbehaves in school. Chances are that his misbehavior is actually being positively reinforced by the attention he receives from his teacher, to say nothing of his classmates. If his behavior is ignored—that is, not reinforced—there is a good chance that it will cease, particularly if the situation can be arranged so that he is given the attention he is seeking after, and *only* after, he behaves in a desired manner.

Of course it is not always possible or desirable to ignore misbehavior. The teacher, moreover, might not be able to control the reinforcement that the misbehaving child receives from his peers. He might have to be threatened with, or actually given, some type of punishment to repress that particular undesired behavior. But punishment or threats are not always necessary, desirable, or effective in correcting a child's behavior and cannot be counted upon to produce permanent extinction. A far more effective way of reducing, if not extinguishing, undesired behavior is to reward desired behavior or to reinforce kinds of behavior (such as sitting in one's seat) that are incompatible with the undesired behavior (leaving the seat and walking around the room).

SCHEDULES OF REINFORCEMENT

One of the problems in trying to bring about desired, or to reduce undesired, behavior has to do with the selection of kinds of reinforcers that are likely to be most effective with particular individuals. Another problem has to do with how much or how often to reinforce. Behavioral psychologists have done and are still doing a great deal of research with this problem. They commonly make a distinction between several possible "schedules" of reinforcement.

When a response is reinforced every time it is made, a continuous schedule is in effect. If, for example, a child is picked up whenever he cries, if he is praised whenever he puts his toys away, if he is told that he is right every time he spells a word correctly, he is receiving continuous reinforcement.

When a response is sometimes reinforced and sometimes not, an intermittent schedule is operative. Intermittent schedules may be either "fixed" or "variable." Fixed schedules are used when the response is reinforced in accordance with a predetermined time-table. If the plan calls for the child to be rewarded only after he has made the desired response a specified number of times, a "fixed ratio" schedule is being used. Complimenting a child not every time he brushes his teeth, but every tenth or twentieth time would be an example of fixed ratio reinforcement.

If the strategy is to reward the child for desired responses regardless of the number of times he makes them, only after a specified period of time has elapsed, a "fixed interval" schedule is in effect. For example, a teacher might have some special treat every Friday afternoon for those students who behaved all week long without being rewarded. The treat is given after they have sat quietly and done their work (or whatever) for the fifth consecutive day.

So-called "variable" schedules of reinforcement are in a sense not really schedules at all. Reinforcement is not given continuously nor in accordance with any set plan. Rather, the frequency of the reinforcement varies from situation to situation and is largely of matter of "playing it by ear." Thus, the intervals between reinforcement or the number of responses needed for reinforcement can be gradually extended. With a "variable ratio" schedule, for example, a child might in the early stages of his learning how to talk be rewarded continuously; then every third time he says "Dada"; then every fifth, or tenth, or twentieth time, etc. With the "variable interval" schedule, there is a similar inconsistency, but with regard to the passing of time rather than the number of responses. The expectation, of course, is that eventually the learner might not have to be formally reinforced at all, or only very rarely.

Formal schedules of reinforcement are more likely to be used in the learning laboratory than in a home or a school. But parents, teachers and others who attempt to change behavior systematically are well advised to experiment with schedules of their own.

GENERALIZATION AND DISCRIMINATION

Behavior that is learned through operant conditioning or classical conditioning or a combination of the two is subject to the processes of generalization and discrimination. These processes help account for the fact that we learn many things that we have not been specifically taught. We are able to do so because we have learned to generalize and to differentiate.

According to the principle of generalization, having learned to respond in a particular way to one particular stimulus, we tend to respond in the same way to similar stimuli. A child who has been reinforced for calling his father "Daddy" is likely to call all adult males by that name until he has learned to discriminate. A person who has been frightened by a German shepherd dog is likely to react with fear to the sight of other kinds of dogs. A person who has found playing tennis or watching a baseball game to be a rewarding experience might, through the process of generalization, acquire an interest in playing golf or watching football games. Thus, the stimuli we experience, the responses we make, and the pleasant or unpleasant effects of those responses can all be transferred to new situations.

Discrimination, of course, is just the opposite of generalization. Through selective reinforcement, the child eventually learns to distinguish his father from other men. He finds that while he might be rewarded for running, jumping, and throwing a ball on the playground, these very same behaviors in the classroom are not appreciated. He learns that the consequences of greeting some people with a friendly "How Ya Doing" are not the same as those of addressing other people in the same way. In short, it is largely through differential reinforcement, along with trial and error as well as imitation, that he learns that all dogs are not equally dangerous, that all foods are not equally tasty, that some people are more reliable than others, that the symbol *b* represents a sound different from that of a *d*, etc.

THE TEACHER'S ROLE

In this chapter we have focused on learning rather than on teaching. In later chapters—especially Chapters 6, 8, and 10, which deal respectively with methodology, motivation, and the individual-ization of instruction—we shall relate some of these behavioral principles of learning to the art (or science) of teaching. We shall consider some ways the teacher can "condition" students to make "desired responses" while respecting their human dignity and in-dividuality. But before going on with the role of the teacher in guiding the learning process, let's summarize some other ways in which learning takes place.

SUMMARY

Much of our behavior—some would say all of it—can be under-stood in terms of conditioning. There are two main forms of con-ditioning: classical and operant. Classical (or respondent) condi-tioning is best illustrated by Pavlov's famous experiment in which a dog "learned" to drool in response to a buzzer. Operant (or instrumental) conditioning is more closely associated with B.F. Skinner and behavioral engineering. Of the two, operant condi-tioning is far more relevant to the work of teachers.

Pavlovian conditioning principles help explain how some of our emotional or affective learning takes place and how a great many of our verbal associations are formed. Simple conditioning along with imitation, for example, goes a long way toward de-scribing how language is learned and how much of our factual information is acquired, at least on a superficial level. While classical conditioning explains many of the automatic, involun-tary responses we have learned to make, operant conditioning is more useful in explaining our voluntary behavior.

The basic principle of operant conditioning is that behavior is shaped, if not actually determined, by its consequences. That is, acts having pleasant consequences tend to be repeated and thus learned, while those having unpleasant consequences tend to be avoided, and thus not learned or unlearned. The key concept of operant conditioning is reinforcement. For new behavior to be learned it must be somehow rewarded or reinforced. Some rein-forcers, such as food, are considered primary. Others are termed secondary or conditioned. Among the latter are money, approval, attention, and particular objects or activities that a person has learned to value.

67

Part of a teacher's job is to see to it that desired forms of behavior are systematically rewarded, and that undesired behaviors are not. This task involves selecting reinforcers that will be effective with particular students, and working out appropriate schedules of reinforcement. While negative reinforcement and punishment can be used to change a person's behavior, positive reinforcement is generally regarded as potentially far more effective. Operant conditioning (or programming) as it relates to classroom instruction is discussed early in Chapter 6.

Recommended Readings

Anderson, Richard, and Faust, G.W. *Educational Psychology.* New York: Dodd Mead, 1973. A partially programmed textbook that illustrates as it explains operant conditioning with special reference to classroom instruction.

Becker, Wesley C. et al. *Teaching 1: Classroom Management.* Chicago: Science Research Associates, 1975. Designed for self-paced individualized study, this book is also partially programed. While explaining the basic principles and concepts of operant conditioning, its emphasis is on classroom management. A very practical book.

Blackham, Garth, and Silberman, Adolph. *Modification of Child and Adolescent Behavior,* 2d ed. Belmont, Cal.: Wadsworth, 1975. A clear explanation of operant conditioning and the techniques of behavior modification with applications to the school and home. The last three chapters deal specifically with a variety of particular behavior problems.

Krumboltz, John D., and Krumboltz, Helen B. *Changing Children's Behavior.* Englewood Cliffs, N.J.: Prentice-Hall, 1972. One of the simplest and clearest introductions to operant conditioning techniques available. Addressed to parents as well as teachers, the book includes numerous examples and practical suggestions.

MacMillan, Donald L. *Behavior Modification in Education.* New York: Macmillan, 1973. A good overview of the subject, not too technical for the beginner, but weighty enough for the somewhat more advanced student. Includes a short discussion of the historical development of behavior modification and some criticisms or shortcomings of that strategy.

Psychology Today, November, 1972. The following articles in this issue are well worth your attention: "It's Time We Taught the Young How to be Good Parents (And Don't You Wish We'd Started a Long Time Ago?)"; "Field Report: Shapers at Work"; "Who's Who and Where in Behavior Shaping"; "Will Success Spoil B.F. Skinner?"; "TV for Kiddies: Truth, Goodness, Beauty—and a Little Bit of Brainwash."

Skinner, B.F. *About Behaviorism.* New York: Random House, 1974. The views of the best known of contemporary behaviorists, and a reply to his critics. Also recommended are his controversial *Beyond Freedom and Dignity* (1971), *Walden Two* (1948, 1962), *and The Technology of Teaching* (1968).

Ulrich, Roger et al., eds. *Control of Human Behavior.* Vol. III. Glenview, Ill.: Scott, Foresman, 1974. A collection of 19 articles dealing with behavior modification in a variety of situations from infancy through adulthood.

Williams, Robert L., and Anandam, Kamala. *Cooperative Classroom Management.* Columbus, Ohio: Charles E. Merrill, 1973. Emphasizes the ethical and social aspects of behavior modification, and recommends teacher-student partnerships in classroom management. Especially recommended is the first chapter in which the authors examine and reply to some of the more common objections to behavior modification.

4

Learning by Discovery and Conceptualization

As was suggested at the beginning of the first chapter, some of the things we have learned were not specifically taught to us. We learned them pretty much on our own through what might be called our own discoveries. For example, without ever having been taught that such is the case, you might have discovered that one of your acquaintances is honest and highly reliable while another is quite the opposite. Or quite by chance you might have discovered a restaurant where the food is particularly well-suited to your taste as well as your pocketbook. Some trial and error might have been involved in such learning experiences, but they would still qualify as genuine discoveries.

THE NATURE OF DISCOVERY

Even some of the outcomes of our schooling are not so much (if at all) the consequences of formal instruction as they are of our own independent discoveries. Without having been formally taught how to study, for example, you might have discovered the time and place and way to study that is best for you. Without any systematic instruction you might have discovered how to receive good grades in a particular course with a minimum of effort. In the chemistry lab you might have "discovered" a principle that had been well-known to professional chemists for years, but perhaps no one had ever told you about it so that it was, in a very real sense, a personal discovery for you.

Similarly you may have discovered that $25 + 10 = 40 - 5$, or that Picasso leaves you cold while Chagall turn you on, or that alleged experts in a given field often disagree among themselves on basic issues within their field. Probably with the help of your teachers, but possibly with little assistance from them at all, you might have discovered what democracy "really means" to you "as a person," or what a particular poem "is really all about." Very likely, either in school or outside of school, you have discovered— or someday will discover—some pretty important things about yourself: your strengths, your weaknesses, your potentialities, etc.

HOW WE DISCOVER

The term *discovery* in the present context refers to those kinds of learning activities which involve relatively little teacher guidance, direction, or deliberate intervention. It implies more than looking something up in a reference book or accidentally stumbling upon some new revelation. But it does imply finding or figuring things out by and for oneself. It is doubtful that anyone ever learns anything completely on his own. But learning by discovery is characterized by the learner's reliance on his own first-hand experiences, his own observations, and exploration based on his own curiosity, his own experimentation, his own analytical and intuitive thinking.

Learning by discovery is essentially a matter of recognizing relationships. Discovery occurs when we come to perceive a situation in a new way, or when we restructure our experience in such a way that new patterns or relationships emerge. It occurs, for example, when we reach our own conclusions or find a new way of doing or interpreting or expressing something. Thus, discovery is part of the problem solving and creative processes, which we shall consider in the next chapter.

We are said to have learned by discovery when, with a minimum of outside help or coaxing, we reorganize our previously acquired information about a subject so that a fuller understanding of that subject is developed. We learn through discovery when we extrapolate our information or draw inferences from it so as to produce new information or deeper insights. It is largely through the discovery process that we formulate our own principles or recognize generalizations without having them pointed out to us. It is through our own discoveries that we eventually arrive at the "personal meaning" of an idea or a principle.

MEANING

Just about everyone, I suppose, would agree that material which is learned should be "meaningful." But what do we mean by meaningful? How does material become meaningful? How can it be made more meaningful?

The meaning of an idea (or an experience) is your understanding of the implications of that idea, your recognition of its relationships to other ideas, your awareness of its significance to you here and now or in the future as you foresee it. In short, meaning as we are presently using that term is a highly personal, individualized matter. In this sense, meaning cannot be transmitted; it must be derived or discovered by the individual himself.

Let's take as an example the Declaration of Independence. Through conditioning procedures a child can rather easily be taught that the Declaration was written by Thomas Jefferson and that it was signed in 1776. If need be, he could memorize the Declaration verbatim. But he still might not have the slightest idea of what "self-evident. . .endowed. . .Creator. . .inalienable rights. . . pursuit of happiness" means. He could, of course, look up the words in a dictionary, or his teacher could define them for him. But his understanding of the Declaration of Independence might still be lacking the kind of meaning presently under discussion.

What about the implications and ramifications of the ideas

contained therein? How do they affect him personally as an American citizen? How, if at all, do they relate to some of the things that are going on in this country or in other parts of the world today? How "sacred" are those ideas? Sacred enough so that he would be willing to fight and if necessary die for them as many of the colonists did? Or are they, after all, just a lot of high-sounding words on an old piece of parchment?

I could tell you what the Declaration of Independence—or religion or music or justice or behavioral psychology—means to me. I can explain my meanings to you and try to persuade you to accept them. But I cannot "give" them to you. You have to discover your meanings for yourself. The meanings which you presently attach to these or any other concepts might have been derived by means of a lengthy chain of simple associations and reinforcement. But at a higher cognitive level the meaning of a particular fact, idea, principle, or experience to an individual depends on such variables as his present interests, needs, values, and goals; on what he has previously learned and presently remembers about the subject or a related subject; and on his particular circumstances at the moment.

THE TEACHER'S ROLE

But what is the teacher's role in all of this? Does he just sit around drinking coffee while his students are off discovering personal meaning? Hardly. In Chapter 6 we shall discuss his role in facilitating the learning process by means of discovery methods. At this point let us simply recognize that cognitive psychologists such as Jerome Bruner, believe that the most important and most uniquely personal knowledge is that which the learner himself discovers. They maintain, therefore, that classroom activities should be planned and organized in such a way that, insofar as possible, the student is not only permitted, but challenged and encouraged to make his own discoveries, either by working independently or with others in small groups.

Classroom learning through discovery, according to Bruner, has several advantages over the more traditional teacher-centered classroom in which the student's main occupation seems to be to sit, listen, receive, accept, assimilate, and remember. He claims, for example, that discovery methods help students learn how to learn or how to acquire information that might be needed in a particular situation later in life. He believes that discovery methods help develop the student's curiosity, sharpen her reasoning abilities and powers of observation, and make her more self-reliant and less dependent upon her teacher or textbook.

Those who hold cognitive theories of learning are convinced that material learned through discovery is better retained, more readily applied, and more viable for problem-solving purposes than that which is transmitted through a more traditional methodology or through sophisticated programming techniques. Discovery methods, they add, involve the student more actively in, and give him a greater responsibility for, his own education. Such learning, they contend, is not only more valuable, but a lot more interesting and a lot more fun than sitting, listening, taking notes, and reciting.

As we shall see, there is no set formula for teaching according to the discovery method, no specific procedures that have to be followed. Discovery methods of teaching or learning by no means exclude the ways of learning discussed in earlier chapters. In fact, what we have been calling learning by discovery could be explained as essentially cases of complex operant conditioning, with heavy doses of trial and error, imitation, and some simple classical conditioning. But to understand more fully the idea of learning through personal discovery, we must take into account a few principles of perception, particularly as they relate to meaning.

PERCEPTION

Perception is the psychological process by which we organize and coordinate and thus interpret or derive meaning from our sensory experiences. As the early Gestaltists pointed out, these experiences, that is, the environmental stimuli we encounter, do not occur as independent, isolated elements. They always appear in some setting, as part of a pattern or configuration. They are always somehow related to other stimuli. Thus, the meaning of a particular object or experience or whatever depends at least in part on its relationships with other objects or experiences and to the "total situation" of which they are parts. Perception is the recognition or awareness of these relationships.

The manner in which we respond to a stimulus depends not only on how we perceive that stimulus but also, quite often, on how we perceive ourselves, our fellow human beings, other stimuli, and the world around us. Perception pertains not only to what a person "sees" in a situation, but also to how he "feels" about it, and what he does as a consequence. In other words, what I do in a given stituation depends not only (and maybe not so much) on what is "out there" in objective reality, but on what is somehow within me, or in my so-called "mind's eye." This, of course, is the principle underlying the idea of beauty residing in the eye of the beholder.

FRAME OF REFERENCE

Midway between the stimuli you experience and the responses you make is you, the individual person, a unique human being. Although you may never have thought of yourself in these terms, you are the "organismic variable" or the "mediating factor" between the S and the R. All that this really means is that you and I do not necessarily respond to the same stimuli in the same way. If you do not believe me, let's you and I go to a rock concert someday. Our responses will very likely differ because before a response is made the stimuli, the sights and sounds and smells and tactile impressions, are organized by—or, as it were, filtered through—different individual human beings.

The manner in which an individual perceives an object or a situation is largely determined by such factors as his previous experience, including his educational background, his age, the condition of his health, his hopes and aspirations, and his sex. All of these and other factors go to make up the individual's frame of reference. Differences in our frames of reference help account for the fact that an experience or an object that is reinforcing to you is not necessarily reinforcing to me, and vice versa.

Because we ourselves are constantly changing and our

environment is constantly changing, our perceptions are constantly changing. Some of the things that we perceived as beautiful or necessary or even desirable when we were ten years old we probably do not perceive in the same way at present. Ten years from now, or even tomorrow, our perceptions are likely to be different from what they are today. These perceptual changes can be thought of as outcomes of learning, while learning itself is sometimes a matter of simply changing one's frame of reference.

SELECTION

Perception is a highly selective process. Ordinarily we attend to or focus on and respond to certain elements of a situation or accentuate some features and ignore or fail to notice others. If I were to meet a bear while strolling through the woods, I doubt that I would notice the species of trees or the color of the vegetation surrounding it. The "only" thing I would see would be the bear itself. Everything else would be literally and figuratively in the background. A few minutes earlier, while I was intent on studying the foliage or simply enjoying the beauties of nature, the trees and shrubs were very much in the foreground. But the bear's arrival on the scene changed all that. If I were to see that very same bear in a different setting, in a circus or a zoo for example, my

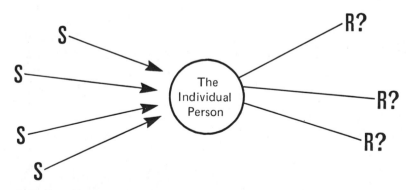

An Individual's Response to the Stimuli He Experiences Depends on His Perception of Those Stimuli

perceptions and reactions would be quite different. So would those of a person with a different frame of reference, such as a hunter or a photographer who was deliberately seeking a bear to pose for him.

Sometimes we "see" in a particular situation only what we want to see or have decided in advance that we are going to see. Thus, we sometimes see things that are not even there, or magnify things that occur only rarely or to a very small degree. Imagine, for example, a high school principal who has already made up her mind that a particular teacher is unable to control his class. She walks into that classroom at a time when twenty-nine of the students are intently doing their work and one is fooling around. Guess which one she will notice?

The devil, it has been said, is able to quote scripture for his own purposes. If this is indeed the case, the devil's behavior can be understood with reference to the selective aspect of the perceptual process. So can the behavior of prejudiced people whose prejudices are confirmed and strengthened when they allow themselves to see only what they expect to see. The same is true of idealists who can only see the good in other people.

One factor that accounts for the individual's perceiving as he does is the reinforcement he receives for doing so. If, for example, it makes me feel good to perceive other people as honest and reliable, I am likely to continue doing so. If, on the other hand, I am somehow reinforced for regarding them as dishonest or unreliable ("It just doesn't pay to trust people.") that very likely is the way I shall continue to perceive them. Thus, many of our present perceptions are responses learned at least in part through operant conditioning. Perceptual selectivity also helps explain the fact that in imitating others, we do not copy or attempt to copy all of another person's behavior, but usually only those particular behaviors that we think will somehow be advantageous to us. Here again the principle of reinforcement seems to be at work.

INSIGHT

Perceptual changes are sometimes thought to come in a flash of what has been called insight. Our sensory experiences, you will recall, are not separate, distinct, mutually exclusive stimuli which are isolated from one another, but are always somehow related to certain other stimuli and are parts of some total situation. Insight is the sudden recognition of the essential relationships in such a situation. It is achieved when the parts fall into place, as it were, and the whole picutre becomes clear. Or at least clearer than it had been.

Insight has been referred to as the Aha! phenomenon. It occurs at the moment when we can truthfully say, "Aha. . .Now I see. . .Comes the dawn!. . .Eureka! I have found it!. . . . Suddenly it's all very clear. . .Now I really understand." Perhaps you can recall working on a puzzle of some sort or on a geometry problem or some other kind of problem with no discernible success, or studying one of your more abstract subjects in high school or college without having the slightest idea of what it was all about. Then it suddenly hit you. "Oh, now I get it." That's insight.

Although insight seems to occur instantaneously in a kind of flash, it is actually the culmination of our previous learning and thinking. When it will come, why it comes and exactly how it comes remain something of a mystery. Insight apparently cannot be engineered; it cannot be hurried or produced on schedule. Like perception and the discovery of meaning, to which it is so closely related, insight is a very personal and individual matter. In helping a student to develop insights, a teacher can apparently take a student just so far. After that, it is pretty much up to him.

CONCEPTUALIZATION

Some of our most important learning—especially the kind that involves discovery, meaning, and understanding—results from our own independent thinking. As we shall see in the next chapter, the processes commonly referred to as thinking take a variety of forms. But the various modes of thinking have at least one thing in common: they all involve the organization or reorganization of concepts. Thus, concepts are indispensable prerequisites for thinking. They are, in fact not only the basic unit of thinking but of practically all verbal or cognitive kinds of learning as well. The process by which we acquire and refine our concepts is appropriately referred to as conceptualization. But what are concepts?

THE NATURE OF CONCEPTS

A concept is essentially an idea or an understanding of what something is. For example, your ideas of what elephants or pencils or lawyers are, or what beauty or carbon dioxide or anthropology is, are among the countless concepts you have already acquired. Your impressions of yourself, your perception of yourself, your idea of who or what you are constitute your concept of yourself, that is, your self-concept.

In certain instances, your concepts might be erroneous or incomplete or at least different from mine. You might have the idea, for example, that a short-stop is a hockey player who tries to stop the small piece of hard rubber short of its entering the net. You and I might have pretty much the same concepts of what pucks and goal-tenders are, but we might not have precisely the same concept of, say, love or even good sportsmanship. Whatever it is that the words love or shortstop mean to you are your concepts of love and shortstop respectively.

A concept is not the same as a word. Words are symbols of concepts or ways of expressing them. Words and concepts are not always or necessarily properly associated. I might have an idea, for example, of a person who specializes in the study of snakes without ever having heard the word herpetologist. On the other hand, I might be able to pronounce and spell herpetology without having any idea of what it means.

A concept is not an image or a mental picture of some particular object. It is, rather, an understanding of or a generalization about a group or class of objects or situations that distinguish them from other groups or classes. Thus, your concept of flower is not limited to any particular flower or kind of flower, but it applies to all flowers regardless of size, shape, color, texture, aroma, species, etc. You undoubtedly have a concept of roses which is narrower than your concept of flowers, and a concept of vegetation or of life that is far broader.

ABSTRACTION

It is through the process of conceptualization that a person is able to organize and thus derive meaning from or make sense out of what would otherwise be a bewildering array of sights, sounds, tastes, smells, people, objects, words, events, and other situations that he experiences. Conceptualization is essentially a matter of organizing or classifying our experiences, or categorizing them by noting similarities and differences, of giving them what has been called "cognitive structure," and often a label or verbal symbol as well.

Conceptualization involves two subprocesses: generalization (or integration) and differentiation (or discrimination.) By means of these subprocesses, we classify objects or situations on the basis of what we perceive as their common or distinguishing characteristics. Generalization and differentiation, in turn, depend upon the abstraction of these elements or characteristics from the total situation.

Very early in life, for example, when the child perceives that bread, milk, meat, and cookies have something in common, he has begun to form, through generalization, the concept of food. He abstracts or pulls out, as it were, whatever it is that distinguishes them from non-food. Temporarily, he ignores the difference between bread and milk or between cookies and carrots, but recognizes that they have something in common that sets them apart from other things such as spoons, cups, or his fist. Such nonessential details as color, taste, etc. are temporarily omitted from consideration. What remains is the essence or "defining element" of food.

The child might not be able to define the word *food* in scientific terms. He might not have learned as yet to say "food." But he has nevertheless an idea of what food is. Later, through further generalization and differentiation, he will develop concepts of

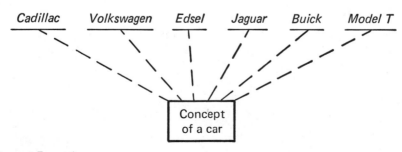

Concept Formation

fruit, vegetable, meat, solid food, liquid food, nutritious food, expensive food, etc. Similarly, he will classify (or conceptualize) non-foods as toys, clothing, cups, paper, etc. By abstracting a certain something from jackets, sweaters, socks, shirts, blouses, parkas, underwear, raincoats, etc., he will place them in a different mental category from, say, knives, forks, spoons, bowls and saucers, which have a different "certain something" in common. This "certain something," of course, is the so-called essence or defining element of the concept *clothing* or *dining utensil.*

Some of our concepts are of situations or qualities which never have been and never can be directly observed. These are referred to as abstract ideas. We cannot, for example, see redness; we can only observe a variety of red objects. We cannot observe beauty in and of itself; but we can observe a variety of objects or situations which have something in common that we have arbitrarily named beauty. We cannot see the numerical abstraction ten; but we can see ten of these, ten of those, and ten of something else. The common element of ten (or red or beautiful) apples, books, noses, cars, suits, or whatever is abstracted, and the result is a concept of ten-ness or redness or beauty. Similarly, from a number of situations in which individuals have been seen to act in a certain way, the common element in their behavior is abstracted and used in the development of such concepts as courtesy or justice or rudeness or delinquency.

THE ROLE OF EXPERIENCE

Conceptualization is a cumulative process. That is, certain kinds of concepts must be grasped before others can be comprehended. Concept formation, then, is largely a process of building upon previously acquired ideas through appropriate forms of guidance and reinforcement. The process presumes previous experience as a requisite.

Children begin to form simple concepts in the first year of life. Long before they have learned to express them verbally, they ordinarily have formed such concepts as warm and cold, pleasure and pain, hunger and thirst, light and dark. Early in life they develop such concepts as chair, table, dog, cat, eyes, ears and nose. But the quality as well as the number and variety of a child's concepts depends on the kinds of experiences he has had.

It is very doubtful that a child who has never seen a dog or even a picture of one will know what dogs are. A child growing up in a slum area will in all probability have quite a different concept of a house than a middle-class suburban child. One raised on a farm is likely to have a better concept of, say, chickens or silos than either of the other two. Since conceptualization is a cumulative, developmental process, with the ideas formed later in life so dependent upon those formed earlier, the child's need for a rich experiential background in his preschool years cannot be over-emphasized from the standpoint of his future cognitive development.

THE TEACHING OF CONCEPTS

One of the most important parts of a teacher's job at every grade level and in practically every subject area is to help students develop new concepts or to clarify or refine concepts they have previously acquired. At the elementary level, for example, the teacher might well be expected to teach such concepts as noun, pronoun, mile, kilometer, insect, volcano, least common denominator, island, peninsula, star, planet, and countless others. Among the numerous concepts taught by a biology teacher we might mention, by way of further example, organism, cell, protoplasm, chlorophyl, epidermis, deoxyribonucleic acid, etc. Among the concepts I have tried to develop in this book are affective objectives, operant conditioning, and perception. I am presently trying to help you arrive at a concept of concepts.

Sometimes concepts can be taught by means of formal definition or verbal explanation. But concept formation is a cumulative process. That is, certain concepts (such as the idea of what a stimulus is, for example) must be grasped before more complex concepts (such as reinforcing stimuli) can be grasped. The process of teaching concepts, then, is largely a matter of building upon and interrelating previously acquired ideas and using previously formed verbal associations. To tell a student that paleontology is the study of fossils, for example, is not likely to be particularly helpful unless he has already acquired a concept of fossils.

In many cases, particularly with younger students, a far more effective way of developing a concept than verbal definition is to have the learner experience the object directly. In trying to arrive at an idea of what a dolphin is, for example, there is no substitute for seeing, touching, listening to and smelling a real, live dolphin. The best way to understand what an earthquake is, I suppose, would be to live through one. But because of the obvious difficulties in producing earthquakes for instructional purposes—or of bringing dolphins to class for "show and tell"—the teacher settles for the next best thing, relying on pictures, models, films, tapes, vivid verbal descriptions, and whatever other materials might be available.

It is usually a good idea to have the learner experience the concept to be learned in a variety of situations and under different circumstances. In learning about trees, for example, it would be beneficial for a child to experience big trees, little trees, palm trees, oak trees, etc., so as to preclude the impression that a tree is necessarily of a certain size, shape or color. To help a student form a concept of a revolution, for another example, he might be led to understand what the American, French, English, and Russian revolutions, the industrial revolution, and various other political, social, cultural, moral, and religious revolutions have in common that warrants their being classed as such despite the differences among them.

A new, unfamiliar concept is often best introduced by relating it to an idea that the learner already possesses. A child might be informed, for example, that a meter is something like a yard or that an adverb is something like an adjective. After the learner has grasped the similarities so that he has at least a general understanding of the new idea, the teacher can point out the differences to help him distinguish it from the old one. In order not to confuse the student with details too soon, the teacher should stress the prominent or essential elements of the concept first. She might emphasize, for example, that sudden change, and not violence, is at the heart of the concept of revolution. Having explained and given a few examples of what a revolution is, she might then ask her students to furnish other examples and discuss the concept so as to arrive at as full an understanding of it as they are capable of at their stage of development.

LANGUAGE

Concepts are ordinarily expressed in words or phrases. Thus, it is through the use of language that a great many of our concepts are acquired, understood, communicated to others, and used to help us form other concepts. Through and only through the use of language a person is able to form concepts of objects or situations that he has not and perhaps could not experience first hand. Most of us, I suspect, have never seen a ghost or a light year or an atom or mental health, but we have at least a general idea of what those words stand for.

As we have seen, a person can have a concept without knowing the accepted name for it. For example, a person might have an understanding of what respondent conditioning is without ever having heard that particular term. Conversely, one might use certain words and even be able to repeat their dictionary definitions without genuinely understanding the ideas they represent. People might talk glibly about love, freedom, democracy, etc., with perhaps only the vaguest notion of what these words mean to the individuals they are addressing or even to themselves. In some cases, we have a fairly clear concept (such as a cow) and we know the word (that is, the arbitrary symbol for) cows, but we might still be hard pressed to explain just exactly what it is that makes a cow a cow and that distinguishes cows from, say, horses or sheep.

A person cannot talk intelligently about cows or democracy or goaltenders or justice or paleontologists unless he knows what they are; what makes them what they are, that is what their essence is; how they differ from other things; and knows the words that by common agreement are used to designate them in its particular culture. Concepts are absolutely essential to cognitive learning and thinking as well as communication, but a problem arises from the fact that words and expressions used to symbolize concepts do not always have the same meaning to different individuals.

Without intruding into the highly specialized and technical area of psycholinguistics, we might recall that most words have connotations as well as denotations, that is, a subjective as well as an objective dimension. The objective dimension, the denotation, is the dictionary definition of a word. The connotation, the subjective dimension, is the set of images, feeling, memories, etc.,

85

that the word brings to mind even though they are not explicitly brought out in or necessary to the definition.

The denotation of the word *mother,* for example, is female parent. If you know what a female is and what a parent is, you know what a mother is. In this regard there is little if any room for doubt, private interpretation or personal meaning. But somehow we still do not think of ourselves as sending a box of candy to our "female parent" on Female Parents Day early in the month of May. The word mother suggests or implies ideas associated with your mother (not mine or anyone else's) that probably extend far beyond that of female parenthood in the strict biological sense. These personal, emotionally-toned images and associations not only constitute the word's connotation; they, rather than the idea of female parenthood, are what prompt us to send the candy. Similarly our responses to other words—money, poison, communist, Jew, teacher, music, automobile, etc.—depend not so much on the denotations as to the connotations of those words.

The learning of language, as we have seen, involves somewhat different processes from those involved in the learning of concepts, even though the two are very closely related. While the learning of language in the sense of associating verbal symbols with objects or concepts can perhaps be satisfactorily explained in terms of imitation and conditioning, the learning of concepts and the connotations of words that represent those concepts seems to be more a matter of perception and personal discovery.

SUMMARY

Some of the most important things we have learned were not intentionally or specifically taught to us. Rather, we learned through our own independent discoveries. Discovery learning is characterized by the individual's reliance on his own observations, experience, perception, experimentation, exploration, and thinking, with a minimum of teacher guidance or intervention.

Learning by discovery is largely a matter of reorganizing our experience, or recognizing new relationships, and coming to perceive things in a new way. It is primarily through our own discoveries that we arrive at the personal meaning of an idea or a principle. Personal meaning cannot be taught in the sense that factual information can be presented. Since it is so subjective, personal meaning can only be derived by and for the individual himself.

Perception is the process by which we organize, interpret, and make sense out of the bewildering array of our sensory experiences. The manner in which we respond to our environment depends not only on how we interpret that environment—the meaning it has for us—but also on how we perceive ourselves in relation to the environment and to other people.

The basic unit of learning—and of thinking, which is discussed in the next chapter—is the concept. A concept is an idea or an understanding of what something is. Concept formation involves the perception of similarities and differences in the objects or situations we experience, and the abstracting of their essential, distinguishing features.

One of the most important parts of a teacher's job at every grade level and in practically every subject area is to help students develop new concepts, and to clarify and refine concepts they have previously formed. In learning new concepts, there is no substitute for first-hand experience. More often than not, however, concepts are learned through the medium of language. Because of the connotations of certain words, language sometimes conceals or distorts meaning.

Conceptualization is a cumulative process. That is, certain simpler concepts usually have to be learned before more complex ones can be understood. When the situation permits, teachers are advised to arrange classroom activities so that the student will be able to discover concepts for himself.

Recommended Readings

Bruner, Jerome, S. *The Relevance of Education.* New York: Norton, 1973. Nine fairly short essays by this well known cognitive psychologist and foremost advocate of learning by discovery. A good overview of his ideas. Also recommended are two of his earlier books, *The Process of Education* (1962), and *Toward a Theory of Instruction* (1966).

Combs, Arthur W. et al. *The Professional Education of Teachers.* 2d ed. Boston: Allyn and Bacon, 1974. Subtitled "A Humanistic Approach to Teacher Preparation," this book sets forth the views of a leading perceptual psychologist on the kinds of teachers needed to facilitate the kinds of learning discussed in this chapter.

Hermann, G. "Learning by Discovery: A Critical Review of the Studies." *Journal of Experimental Education,* Fall, 1969. Offers evidence derived from research in support of discovery learning and indicates conditions under which it can be facilitated.

Morine, Harold, and Morine, Greta. *Discovery: A Challenge to Teachers.* Englewood Cliffs, N.J.: Prentice-Hall, 1973. A very practically oriented book that explains and illustrates how discovery methods can be used in the classroom.

Read, Donald A., and Simon, Sidney B. eds. *Humanistic Education Sourcebook.* Englewood Cliffs, N.J.: Prentice-Hall, 1975. A collection of articles on the basic theory and practical implications of humanistic education.

Silberman, Melvin L. et al., eds. *The Psychology of Open Teaching and Learning.* Boston: Little, Brown, 1972. Subtitled "An Inquiry Approach," this book of readings includes several articles on student centered education, discovery, and related topics.

Smith, Frank. *Comprehension and Learning.* New York: Holt, Rinehart and Winston, 1975. Written from the standpoint of cognitive psychology, this book discusses the mental processes of children and shows how they "make sense of the world." Among the topics discussed are language, learning to speak and read, meaningfulness and memorization, and differences among students that affect their comprehension.

Treffinger, Donald J. "Teaching for Self-Directed Learning: A Priority for the Gifted and Talented." *The Gifted Child Quarterly*, Spring, 1975. A very short article that explains what self-directed learning is, why it is so important for brighter students, and how it can be implemented.

Wendel, Robert, "Inquiry Teaching: Dispelling the Myths." *Clearing House,* Spring, 1973. A short article setting forth a balanced view of what the author calls "reflective" teaching and learning.

5

Learning
through Thinking

Thus far we have seen that certain kinds of learning result from imitation, trial and error, respondent or operant conditioning, discovery, perception, concept formation, or a combination of some and very often all of these processes. But there are still other ways of learning. These involve a variety of related but different kinds of mental activities that are commonly, and sometimes loosely, called thinking.

Down through the ages, from ancient times onward, philosophers and psychologists have never agreed as to exactly what thinking is or how it takes place. I do not, therefore, pretend that what I will be saying in this chapter is by any means the final word on the subject. But I welcome this opportunity to help you do some thinking about—thinking.

WHAT IS THINKING?

Not being sure what the word *think* means, I looked it up in a couple of dictionaries. The following is a partial list of some of the synonyms I found: believe, cogitate, conceive, deliberate, expect, fancy, imagine, intend, meditate, plan, ponder, predict, realize, reason, reflect, remember, and speculate. Checking to find how psychologists use the term in a more technical sense, I observe that some seem to regard thinking as synonymous with problem solving. But what some call problem solving, others call reflective thinking, or critical thinking, or reasoning. Some distinguish between problem solving and creative thinking; others use those two terms synonymously, etc.

The word *think*, then, is used popularly as well as technically in a variety of ways to refer to a variety of activities. In this respect, it is similar to the word *play*. We might, for example, play basketball, play pinochle, or play charades. We might play the guitar, play chess, or play the part of Hamlet. We might play hide-and-go-seek, play with a dog, with a model airplane, with a computer, etc. Obviously the word *play* does not mean precisely the same thing in all of these contexts.

Similarly, the thinking that we do in recalling our past experiences is not quite the same as the thinking we do in planning the future. The thinking that one does in solving a mathematical problem is not quite the same as that which goes into, say, solving a personal problem or thinking how nice it would be if we had a million dollars. The thinking that goes into writing a poem is not quite the same as that which is involved in evaluating a poem. The thinking involved in deciding which candidate to vote for is not quite the same as thinking about the beauty of nature or the meaning of life. It would seem, however, that all of these mental activities have something in common that enables us to refer to them with the same word.

For our purposes, thinking can be defined as the organization of concepts, or the rearrangement of ideas, or restructuring of experience—all of which mean essentially the same thing. But concepts can be rearranged in different ways for different purposes, which is why we have different forms or modes of thinking, as we do of learning.

CONVERGENT AND DIVERGENT THINKING

Educators and psychologists generally accept a distinction between what has been called convergent and divergent thinking.

Convergent thinking is so called because it occurs when we reorganize our ideas, drawn perhaps from several different sources, so that they converge at or point unequivocally to *the* one right answer or *the* best solution or *the* only valid conclusion. Thus, convergent thinking takes place only when there *is* one right or best answer. We do not know the answer to begin with, but usually somebody does. One definite correct conclusion is at least possible. What we have to do is "figure it out" by reorganizing the information at our disposal.

Divergent thinking pertains to situations in which there is no one right or best answer. If there is, no one knows it or not everyone agrees on it. Thus, in divergent thinking we reorganize our ideas so as to produce two or more (often several) possible answers or conclusions or solutions or hypotheses, none of which is necessarily "right" or better than any of the others.

Convergent thinking is perhaps best illustrated with a mathematical problem for which there is one right answer with no ifs ands or buts. Divergent thinking would be better illustrated with a social problem. Beginning with all the facts we might have about

THE DIFFERENCE BETWEEN CONVERGENT AND DIVERGENT THINKING

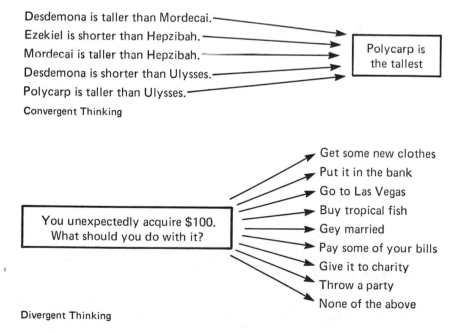

Desdemona is taller than Mordecai.
Ezekiel is shorter than Hepzibah.
Mordecai is taller than Hepzibah.
Desdemona is shorter than Ulysses.
Polycarp is taller than Ulysses.

Polycarp is the tallest

Convergent Thinking

You unexpectedly acquire $100. What should you do with it?

Get some new clothes
Put it in the bank
Go to Las Vegas
Buy tropical fish
Gey married
Pay some of your bills
Give it to charity
Throw a party
None of the above

Divergent Thinking

the crime problem, for example, we might come up with several possible solutions or strategies for dealing with it. But we would not have mathematical certainty or proof that any of the possibilities would get the desired results. Divergent thinking is essentially the same as creative thinking. We will return to it later in this chapter under that heading.

DEDUCTION

Convergent thinking is essentially the same as deductive reasoning, logical thinking, or the deduction of inferences. Deduction takes place when we reorganize our ideas or our existing store of knowledge so as to produce new knowledge, or to uncover or discover some truth or some conclusion of which we were previously unaware. We deduce, for example, that if this is true and if that is true, then something else must necessarily be true. Or we infer that if this is true, then something else is definitely not true. Or probably not true. The truth or the conclusion is "there." All we have to do is rearrange our data so that it will become clear enough for us to recognize it.

To illustrate the process of deductive reasoning (or, if you prefer, convergent thinking) as well as the principle of rearranging ideas, let's consider a problem requiring this type of mental activity.

I know three sisters named Mary, Jean, and Susan. One is a blonde, one a brunette, and one a redhead, but not necessarily in the order named. The shortest girl is the brightest of the three, but is not as pretty as Susan. Jean is younger than the redhead. Mary is older than the brunette. The brunette is neither the tallest nor the oldest, but she's prettier than Jean. The blonde is shorter than the redhead and younger than the dullest of the three. The oldest is the least pretty, but she's a lot brighter than the prettiest one.

Now tell me which girl has what color hair, and rank the

three as to age, height, brightness, and prettiness. All the necessary information is there. All you have to do is reorganize it. You might begin by noting that Jean is not the redhead. Jean, you were informed, is younger than the redhead. Neither is Jean the brunette. The brunette, you will recall, is prettier than Jean. And so forth.

Unlike inductive reasoning, which we shall take up next, deductive reasoning leads to absolute certitude. Assuming that the above statements are true, your inference that Jean is the blonde is indisputably valid. She has to be the blonde. No doubts about it. The conclusion we drew about the color of Jean's hair is, in a sense, not new. Perhaps it was new to you, but it had been "there" right along. It was concealed, as it were, or implicit in the data. Through logical reasoning you made it explicit, just as Sherlock Holmes, through his brilliant deductions, identifies the criminal, or a geometrician, through his deductions, concludes something or other about the size of angles in a triangle.

INDUCTION

We learn through the inductive method of reasoning (or of drawing inferences) by reaching conclusions after a careful examination of particular cases, or by formulating generalizations derived from the study of specific, usually concrete, data. This is why induction is sometimes defined as reasoning from the particular to the general.

Induction is commonly referred to as the scientific method of thinking. Most of the principles and generalizations in the field of psychology, for example, are based on inductive methods. Although scientists do, of course, make great professional use of deduction, their laws and hypotheses are typically based on systematic observations of particular cases. Ordinarily it is impossible to study each and every particular case of the phenomenon under investigation. The psychologist, for example, could not possibly observe every retarded child in the country, or every adolescent or every set of twins. And he need not. Using appropriate sampling procedures, inferential statistics, experimentation, analogy, etc., he can induce conclusions which are applicable to twins, adolescents or retarded children in general.

While deductive reasoning leads to logical certitude, inductive reasoning does not. Induction yields only varying degrees of probability. Thus, a scientist can be confident that his generalizations are true or that they apply in up to 99.99% of the cases, but rarely, if ever, in 100% of them.

One need not, of course, be a scientist in order to reason inductively. It is, in fact, largely through induction that concepts are formed, as we saw in Chapter 4. It is also through induction that concepts are related to one another and that judgments are made. Having arrived at a concept of a dog, for example, a very young child observes that this dog barks, that dog barks, and the other dogs he has seen bark. On the basis of this first-hand, but very limited, experience, he induces the generalization that all dogs bark. In inducing, we reach conclusions which extend beyond the available evidence, but toward which the evidence points. Induction, you will recognize, is the mode of thinking that plays such a central role in the discovery method of learning.

ERRORS

Both inductive and deductive forms of reasoning are, of course, subject to error. In trying to improve our own thinking, therefore, we must guard against the possibility of such errors creeping into and distorting our thought processes. Similarly, in attempting to improve the quality of his students' thinking, one of the principal means that a teacher can employ at any grade level is to guide them toward a recognition of errors in their thinking and in that of others.

Some of these errors or so-called fallacies are of a technical nature involving violations of the rigid rules of logic. For example, from the premises "All Democrats are honest," and "George is a Republican," one simply may not conclude that George is therefore dishonest, even if it were true (which, of course, it isn't) that all Democrats are indeed honest. Even if all Democrats were honest, this would not preclude some (or all) Republicans from being honest, too.

Some errors result from an intrusion of one's feelings or

wishes into the thinking process, or from a simple failure to consider cold, hard facts. Some result from hasty generalization or from the drawing of a conclusion from too small a number of cases, or from situations that are atypical. Maybe I would like to believe that all Democrats (or Republicans, or college professors, or Episcopalians or whatever) are honest; maybe I could name several of them who are; maybe I do not personally know of, and have never heard of, a single exception. But I am still not justified in holding the premise that all members of that group are honest. We must be very careful, therefore, with such so-called universal terms as all, none, always, and never, using them sparingly, if at all; we should favor instead such qualifying terms as some, many, usually, probably, etc.

CRITICAL THINKING

Some of our learning results from a mode of thinking that includes, but goes beyond, inductive and deductive reasoning. This form of thinking occurs when we reorganize our ideas so as to evaluate something: an object, a person, a situation, a proposition, or whatever. It also occurs when we make a judgment as to the relative value of two or more alternatives. This form of thinking is what is ordinarily meant by making up one's own mind or deciding for oneself. I shall be referring to this type of mental activity as critical thinking.

Critical thinking can be distinguished from the drawing of inferences by the element of decision making, or the making of a judgment as to what is good, better, best, or most appropriate in a given situation. Critical thinking necessarily involves inference, as we shall see, but inference does not necessarily imply critical thinking. In the problem involving the three sisters, for example, you might have inferred (correctly) that Susan is the prettiest, Jean the brightest, and Mary the oldest. But so far there has been no critical thinking, no value judgments. If you are a male reader, I hope you have not evaluated them as good prospective dates, since I forgot to tell you that Susan is only seven years old, Jean is eleven, and Mary is eighteen. You are engaged in critical thinking when, for example, you are trying to decide which candidate to vote for, or when you compare candidates' platforms and credentials. Similarly, when you are in the process of making a decision as to what courses to take, what kind of car to buy, which dress to wear on a particular occasion, or which theory of learning to accept, you are thinking critically. Although it might not sound very romantic, even when deciding whom to date, or whom to marry, or whether to get married at all, you are—or should be—doing some critical thinking.

Decisions such as these, of course, are often made largely on the basis of one's feelings at the moment, and have little or nothing to do with the intellectual process under discussion. Some of our decisions result from some type of external pressure. Some might be due primarily to imitation, or habit, or previous conditioning. But when and if our decisions are based on careful intellectual deliberation or logical reasoning, critical thinking has been going on.

EVALUATION

In evaluating anything, we need some sort of standard, some set of criteria, on which to base our judgment. Ordinarily, it is through the process of induction that we formulate our criteria. We apply those criteria to particular cases through the process of deduction.

For example, on the basis of our own experience and observation, and possibly through experimentation or some other form of research, we might conclude inductively that x, y, and z are the only really essential characteristics of effective teachers. For purposes of this example, x, y, and z can stand for anything you wish: knowledge of subject matter, love of children, patience, or what have you. Whoever has these qualities is a good teacher; whoever lacks them is not. The more one has of these traits, the better a teacher that person is.

Applying these criteria to individual teachers, we might observe that Ms. Smith has these qualities; we deduce, therefore, that she is a good teacher. But Mrs. Brown has them to an even greater degree, so we infer that she is a better teacher. We might find that Mr. Jones excels the others with respect to criteria x (he knows his subject matter better than the other two, for example); but Ms. Smith excels with respect to criterion y (she has more patience, a more pleasant personality, or whatever). In this case, we have to arrange our criteria in some sort of hierarchical order by making a decision as to the relative importance of each. Without such an ordering of criteria against which to measure and compare particular cases we are really in no position to evaluate anything.

PROBLEM SOLVING

Just as inductive and deductive reasoning are necessary for making evaluations, so is evaluation a necessary "sub-process" in problem solving. As you may recall, we touched on the problem solving process in Chapter 2 where it was described as a kind of symbolic trial and error means of learning. In terms that have been used in this chapter, problem solving can be defined as the reorganization of concepts so as to overcome some difficulty (or obstacle) and attain some goal. It is characterized by a conscious, deliberate striving for an answer, or a conclusion, or a solution that an individual needs in order to achieve some goal or attain some purpose. The selection of his goals from among a great many possibilities and his decisions as to which of one or more possible means he should use to achieve his goals involve critical thinking.

The kinds of problems one attempts to solve depends on her particular circumstances, level of maturity, and life style. Back in Chapter 2 we saw that one of Becki's major problems at age 15 was how to win friends and satisfy some of her social needs. At an earlier stage of her development, one of her problems might have been to persuade her parents to buy her a toy machine gun, or to get out of having to dry the dishes, or to prepare an interesting presentation for Show and Tell. At a later stage of her development, a major problem might be how to teach an unruly class, balance the family budget, or alleviate racial tensions in her neighborhood.

Note that in each of these situations, there is some obstacle to the immediate attainment of Becki's goal. She either lacks the knowledge necessary for the solution of her problem, in which case she must first acquire it; or she has not properly organized the information she does have, in which case she must reorganize it; or something else stands in the way of reaching out and getting the friends, or the machine gun, or the racial harmony she wants. There is at the moment no obvious, clearly perceived means of reaching her goal. There is no pat, ready-made solution that can be directly applied. Previously acquired behaviors are inadequate in her present situation. Customary or habitual ways of responding will not suffice. If they do, there is no difficulty to be overcome, no problem to be solved, no need for her to tax her mental energies with the process under discussion.

Some problems or apparent problems can, of course, be solved simply by drawing on our memories and applying old solutions to new situations. Ordinarily, when a problem arises that we are not sure how to handle, the first thing we do is try to recall what we did in similar circumstances in the past. We are also likely to make use of imitation, observing what others do in the same or a similar situation. Sometimes we act impulsively, emotionally, using perhaps a random trial and error approach with little or no deliberation. But sometimes we attack our problems logically and systematically, with a well-planned, carefully conceived strategy. It is this approach that I would like to have us examine somewhat more closely.

ANALYSIS OF THE PROCESS

The problem solving process rarely proceeds in a neat, orderly sequence with one concept leading directly to the next and so on to a conclusion. It is, rather, a disorderly process involving more than a little of what we called symbolic trial and error. For purposes of analysis, however, we can distinguish five "steps" in the process as though they did take place one at a time.

First, there is the recognition and definition or delimitation of the problem itself. This step requires an awareness of ways in which our existing situation is somehow in need of improvement, or a sensitivity to defects or shortcomings in ourselves or the world around us. It implies that we pinpoint as clearly and precisely as possible what the real problem is, that we penetrate to the heart of the problem, and that we not allow ourselves to be side-tracked by extraneous, irrelevant issues. In trying to make $10 last us until next payday, for example, our immediate problem is not "what is wrong with the country's economic system" or "why professional athletes are paid so much more than teachers are" but "what I can avoid buying until my financial condition is improved."

Quite often a big problem has to be broken down into a number of component sub-problems. In thinking about "the crime problem," for example, instead of looking for one overall general solution, we might do better to distinguish between violent and nonviolent crime, between organized crime and crime in the streets, between crime on this street and crime on that street, between vandalism on this street and burglaries on the same street. While there may be no simple solution to the problem of "Saturday night muggings on Elm Street by high school students who are on dope," a problem thus narrowly defined stands a better chance of being solved than the global problem of crime in general.

The second step involves gathering and organizing the necessary facts or information. This implies, among other things asking appropriate questions, knowing what kinds of data are needed or are likely to be helpful, and where and how such information can be obtained. It also implies the weighing of evidence and the discrimination between facts on the one hand and opinions or guesses on the other. This, of course, is where inductive and deductive reasoning, as well as a broad and deep store of knowledge about the problem area, a rich experiential background, and skills in research are likely to come in handy.

The third step is the formulation of hypotheses. A hypothesis, as we have previously seen, is a tentative or possible solution to a problem based on the information that is presently at hand. We referred to hypotheses as hunches or educated guesses that if this is done, that will follow. If I stop smoking, I can stretch my $10. If the town declares an 11 o'clock curfew, muggings will decrease. Hypothesizing, in short, is the planning of one's strategy for an attack on a problem. It can also be thought of as narrowing down the field of search in which a solution is likely to be found. Having lost a favorite pipe, for example, instead of looking for it at random all over the campus, I try to recall where I saw it last and hypothesize that if I look in Professor Anderson's office, my pipe and I will be reunited.

Overlapping with the third step is the fourth, the testing or the verification of hypotheses. This is essentially an attempt to foresee as many as possible of the probable consequences of a particular course of action. A chess player, for example, hypothesizes that if he moves a particular pawn to a particular square, he will be in a position to take one of his opponent's knights. But before actually making the move, he tries it out mentally. What else might happen? He might perceive that if he makes that move, his opponent might make a move endangering his own bishop. But if he does that, then I'll be able to take his queen. But if I do that, then I'll be checkmated.

In the case of looking for my pipe, I can easily test my hypothesis overtly by walking next door to my colleague's office. If the pipe is not there, I can form another hypothesis and look elsewhere. But the chess player ordinarily does not have such second or third chances. So before making his move overtly, he is well advised to try it out "in his mind."

The final step is the formulation of a conclusion. If the hypothesis passes the test and is found to be satisfactory, the problem is solved, or at least a course of action has been selected. Otherwise, we might have to go all (or part) of the way back and start all over again, perhaps by redefining our problem, by gathering additional information or reorganizing the information we do have, or by formulating and reformulating, testing and retesting new hypotheses.

Ordinarily, the more hypotheses we can come up with, the greater the chance that one of them will lead to the solution of the problem. The ability to formulate a great number and variety of hypotheses, incidentally, is a good example of what we referred to earlier in this chapter as divergent thinking. Divergent thinking, as we have seen, is another name for creative thinking, which we shall be taking up shortly. For the present, let's simply recognize the part that creativity plays in the problem solving process.

INTUITION

Problems are sometimes said to be solved either analytically or intuitively. The analytic method involves careful, systematic, logical, step by step inductive and/or deductive reasoning. It implies, among other things, a healthy respect for factual data, a weighing of evidence, and the scrupulous observance of the laws of logic. If computers are able to think in the sense of solving problems, it is this type of analytical thinking or data processing that they can be made to do.

Intuitive thinking does not proceed in accordance with well-defined steps such as those we have just discussed. It skips steps, so to speak. It takes short cuts. It bypasses the laborious processes of gathering and weighing evidence. It defies the laws of logic. It is a highly subjective experience wherein the individual "leaps" in some mysterious manner from what he knows or feels directly to a solution, or at least to a plausible hypothesis.

Intuition really does not explain, but it does describe, the situation in which a person "knows" something to be true, or is certain that a particular course of action will get the desired results, without being able to prove his position, offer any evidence in support of it, or demonstrate to anyone else's satisfaction how he arrived at it. He "just knows."

Intuition is the least understood of the various modes of thinking that have been, or will be, discussed. It is, in a sense, a guess or a hunch based more on feeling than on cold, hard reasoning. But the guess often turns out to be right. Intuition has been variously attributed to luck, to chance, to accident, to supernatural forces, to the so-called genetic memory of the human race, to extrasensory perception, to the accumulation and assimilation of ordinary learning experiences, etc. But no one knows for sure why or how it works.

CREATIVE THINKING

Thus far we have seen that human beings can and do learn through a variety of thinking processes. Among these processes are the modes of thinking that we have referred to as intuition, deduction, induction, critical thinking, and problem solving. Still another kind of thinking process is that which is called creative or divergent. It is called creative because it involves the reorganization of ideas so as to produce something new, something which previously did not exist, at least in the mind of the thinker. It is regarded as divergent, rather than convergent, because the reordering of ideas leads not to the one right answer, but to several possible conclusions or new products.

Creative thinking is the process by which we invent or discover a new way of doing something, or of expressing something. It occurs when we relate ideas in a manner in which they ordinarily are not related, or have not been previously related. When Robert Burns compared a certain woman of whom he was very fond to a "red, red rose," he was, in a sense, evaluating her. But his famous line of poetry is more commonly considered a product of creative than critical thinking.

To the extent that they lead to new insights, understandings, hypotheses, conclusions or whatever, the other modes of thinking that we have discussed all involve an element of newness. One of the distinguishing characteristics of creative thinking is that it includes considerably more in the way of novelty, originality, and imagination. Unlike the other modes, creative thinking is not restricted by facts, need not conform to reality, cares not about evidence, and may violate the rules of logic with impunity. When used in connection with problem solving, however, as it frequently is, creative thinking must come down to earth and take reality into account.

Compared with analytic problem solving, critical thinking and the inductive or deductive methods of drawing inferences, creative thinking is far more personal, systematized or structured. The products of creative thinking are not judged as right or wrong, true or false, valid or invalid. They are, rather, evaluated as good or bad, beautiful or ugly, useful or useless, or somewhere on a continuum between those poles.

Creativity is usually associated with such fine arts as writing, painting, musical composition, etc. But it also plays (or can play) an important part in business, engineering, teaching, cooking, and just about any other field of human endeavor. Creative thinking need not result in a lyric poem or an abstract sculpture. Something as commonplace as a meat loaf, a bulletin board display, a garden, or a better mouse trap might be a product of creative thinking, or what is sometimes called creative problem solving.

STAGES OF CREATIVITY

Creative thinking, by its very nature, is a highly individualized process. It follows no prescribed pattern, no set of rules, no formula, no timetable. It does, however, seem to include four identifiable stages.

First there is the preparation stage. This is the period during which the individual gathers her data, forms concepts, and stores up experiences she will later cast into a new form. During this stage, she might deliberately and systematically prepare herself for a creative project she is planning by doing library research, for example, visiting places or interviewing people whom she thinks can help her. The individual might also prepare herself in a far less formal manner by simply observing her environment and keeping herself open to as many new experiences as possible.

The second stage, commonly called the incubation stage, is essentially a period of assimilation. During this stage, there is no visible activity on the part of the thinker. To all outward appearances, she might be making no progress whatsoever. The writer, for example, sits staring at the blank sheet of paper in her typewriter, but nothing clicks. So maybe she goes out for coffee, or maybe she goes back to the library to do some more research. This stage might be of only momentary duration, but it could last for years. During this period, the artist's ideas are lying dormant, as it were, waiting to be hatched. If asked what she is waiting for, she might respond with the word: inspiration.

The third stage, illumination, is no better understood than intuition, to which it is probably somehow related. This stage sometimes comes on gradually, but often it is of only momentary duration, beginning rather dramatically with a sudden flash of insight, sometimes when it is least expected. All at once, it seems, the parts fall into place and a new relationship is perceived. Our writer friend, for example, "gets" her inspiration, which seems to come to her like the proverbial bolt out of the blue. Actually, of course, this apparently sudden enlightenment is the culmination of the two previous stages.

The final stage has been referred to as the verification stage or the expression stage. During this period, the creative thinker tries out her new arrangement of ideas almost as though they were hypotheses. She gets ideas down on paper or on canvas, or actually whips up a new kind of omelette or constructs the new bulletin board. This stage, then, pertains to the actual "making" of the product. In the case of the writer, this involves the actual writing, editing, rewriting, polishing, revising, etc. It might involve tearing up and throwing away countless sheets of paper until they attain a form that she considers satisfactory. In evaluating her own accomplishments, the creative thinker is, of course, doing critical thinking and problem solving as well.

REFLECTIVE THINKING

Despite the theoretical differences among inductive and deductive reasoning, critical and creative thinking, intuitive and analytic problem solving, these are not separate and distinct, mutually exclusive forms of mental activity. In practice, they overlap more likely than not, and are so closely interrelated that it is often difficult to disentangle them. This is one reason why different writers use different terminology to describe the thinking processes.

Some authorities, as we have seen, use the terms problem solving and critical thinking interchangeably. Some use the term reflective thinking to designate one or the other or both. I am not deliberately trying to confuse you with this array of terminology. I am, however, trying to report differences among psychologists, not only with respect to the terms they employ, but also regarding their views of what thinking is and how it takes place.

By the term reflective thinking I mean the mental activity, or the rearrangement of concepts, by which we reflect on an idea without necessarily making any decision or value judgment about it, and without necessarily having any problem to solve. This mode of thinking corresponds to what is sometimes called meditation or contemplation. Reflective thinking occurs when we "mull over" an idea, examining it from many possible angles. We try to perceive the implication, or the applications, or the ramifications of the idea. Using love or freedom as an example, we try to arrive at a fuller, deeper understanding of the idea. We try to find the significance or the personal meaning of the idea. We seek to relate the idea to ourselves and to our particular goals, aspiration, or style of life. Reflective thinking happens when we "think about" a poem, for example, or God, or the meaning of life.

I cannot draw a line indicating where problem solving ends and reflective thinking begins. Perhaps the difference is mainly one of the thinker's intent. When a person deliberately and systematically sets out to find a solution to a problem, it seems that he is engaged in a different type of mental activity than that which has just been described. By whatever name this latter mode of thinking is called, and however it might be related to or different from other modes that we have considered, it does represent yet another way of learning.

SUMMARY

Most of us are inclined, I believe, to react positively to the word *thinking*. As students, we like to do our own thinking, at least once in a while. As teachers, we might want to encourage and help our students do their own thinking. But what do we mean by thinking? What does a person do when he thinks?

The word thinking is used in a variety of ways to refer to a variety of kinds of mental acitivities. Among the more commonly recognized of these are convergent and divergent thinking, inductive and deductive reasoning, critical thinking and problem solving, intuitive, creative, and reflective thinking. All of these involve the rearrangement of concepts or the reordering of experience, but in different ways for different purposes.

The creative thinking that goes into the writing of a poem, for example, is not the same as the critical thinking we might use in evaluating a poem that someone else has written, or for that matter one of our own. The logical, analytical, convergent thinking necessary for the solution of a math problem is different from the reflective thinking we might do about, say, the meaning of love.

Although the various forms of thinking can be separated for purposes of discussion, in practice they ordinarily do not occur singly apart from all of the others. A complete act of problem solving, for example, is likely to include most, if not all, of the other varieties. The same is true of critical thinking. Thus, it is not always possible or necessary to specify the point at which one begins and the other ends.

As we shall see more clearly in the next chapter, learning or teaching others how to think is not a single, simple process because thinking itself takes so many interrelated forms. Just as the various forms of thinking overlap with one another, so do they overlap with and commonly presume the other forms of learning discussed in earlier chapters.

Recommended Readings

Carbone, Peter F. "Objective Morality—Teaching Students to Think Critically." *National Association of Secondary School Principals Bulletin,* Jan., 1975. Maintains that high schools should help students learn to think critically about moral problems. Proposes a course for this purpose that would treat the problems objectively.

Crutchfield, Richard S. "Nurturing the Cognitive Skills of Productive Thinking." In H.F. Clarizio et al., eds. *Contemporary Issues in Educational Psychology.* 2d ed. Boston: Allyn and Bacon, 1974. Discusses the development of skills in four main areas: problem discovery and formulation, organizing and processing information, the generation of ideas, and the evaluation of ideas.

Dewey, John. *How We Think.* Boston: D.C. Heath, 1933. Subtitled "A Restatement of the Relation of Reflective Thinking to the Educative Process," this book is properly regarded as a classic on the subject of problem solving. Serious students of the subject might also wish to read his *Logic: The Theory of Inquiry* (1938). For an easier introduction to Dewey, I would recommend his *Experience and Education* (1938).

Elkind, David. *Children and Adolescents: Interpretive Essays on Jean Piaget.* New York: Oxford University Press, 1970. Of the many books attempting to explain Piaget's theories in simple language and to relate them to classroom instruction, this is one of the clearest and most practical.

Getzels, J.W., and Jackson, P.W. *Creativity and Intelligence.* New York:

John Wiley, 1962. This widely-quoted book includes an explanation, with documentation, of the authors' thesis that creativity is relatively independent of IQ.

Guilford, J.P. *The Nature of Human Intelligence.* New York: McGraw-Hill, 1967. An important source of information about various forms of convergent and divergent thinking, how they can be measured, how they are related to cognition, memory, and evaluation, and to the overall structure of the human intellect.

Imhelder, Barbel, and Piaget, Jean. *The Growth of Logical Thinking.* New York: Basic Books, 1958. A rather technical book, based on Piaget's famous experiments, describing the changes in the logical processes of an individual from childhood through adolescence. Before attempting this or any of Piaget's other books, you are advised to read Elkind or one of the other "introduction to Piaget" books.

Newell, Allen, and Simon, Herbert A. *Human Problem Solving.* Englewood Cliffs, N.J.: Prentice-Hall, 1972. Using a neurological, computer simulation approach, the authors discuss problem solving as an information processing system involving receptors, processors, memory, and effectors.

6

Guiding the Learning Process

So far we have considered various ways of learning. Now let's consider some ways of teaching, some means of helping other people learn. Although we have made a number of references to teachers in earlier chapters, in this one we shall focus on their activities more directly.

Just about everyone agrees on the need for good teachers. Many maintain that a school is only as good as its teachers, and that the quality of the teaching to which a student is exposed is the most critical single factor in determining how much and how well he learns. But what is a good teacher? How can we recognize one? How can we identify truly outstanding teachers and distinguish them from others who are barely mediocre or downright inadequate? To questions such as these there is no generally accepted answer. There never has been and it is most unlikely that there ever will be. Despite the tons of research that have been turned out on the subject, school administrators, board members, professors of education, parents, teachers, and students continue to disagree among themselves and with one another.

Some insist that good teachers are characterized by certain personality traits: patience, kindness, friendliness, warmth, etc. Others hold that far more crucial than qualities such as these are the teacher's skills or competencies. Some are convinced that the most valid, if not the only valid, test of a teacher's competence is how much and how well his students learn.

With respect to the methods they employ in guiding the learning process, the above mentioned tons of research have also failed to reveal any particular kind of methodology that, in and of itself, is necessarily better than any other. A method of teaching reading, for example, that works wonders for one teacher sometimes falls flat with another. A method of teaching math that works well for the same teacher in one school with certain kinds of students might not work nearly as well in another school with other kinds of students. And even with the same teacher in the same school with the same group of students, a method that proves to be highly effective in one subject area is often disastrous in another. So there is no "one best way" of teaching, guaranteed to work or double your money back.

As a propsective teacher you will be (if you have not already been) exposed to a variety of possible methods of teaching particular subjects. In the final analysis, it will be up to you to decide which you want to try in your particular situation. To help you decide, let's consider three general approaches, or so-called strategies, that correspond respectively to the kinds and ways of learning discussed in the last three chapters: conditioning, discovery, and thinking.

TEACHING AS PROGRAMMING

The principles of learning through conditioning are, as we have seen, derivatives of behavioral psychology. From the standpoint of contemporary behaviorism, education is essentially a matter of behavior modification. A good teacher is, above all, a kind of behavioral engineer or a behavior "shaper." Since most, if not all, learning involves conditioning, the teacher's job is to condition people, or program them, to make "desired responses" and to avoid "undesired responses." The purpose of instruction, in short, is to train people to behave in certain predetermined ways, to improve their behavior, so as to produce a better lot of human beings.

In the preceding paragraph, I have deliberately used a few key words which I suspect might annoy you. Perhaps you are repelled by the very idea of conditioning or training or programming people, or of attempting to "produce" human beings who will fit a predetermined set of specifications as though they were so many automobiles coming off an assembly line. Perhaps you have been, if you will pardon the expression, "conditioned" to associate the terminology of behaviorism with the manufacture of robots, or with brain-washing people so that they will do whatever some diabolical mind-manipulating Big Brother out of *1984* wants them to do. Perhaps because of the impersonal connotations of the term, you cannot or will not think of yourself as a prospective behavioral engineer.

If the jargon of behaviorism bothers you, do not use it. Instead of the term *behavioral engineer,* for example, you might prefer to use the term *learning facilitator* or simply the good old word *teacher.* Instead of the verb *condition,* you might feel more comfortable with something like *instruct* or *guide* or *direct* or *inform.* Any of these can be used as a substitute for the verb *program* as well.

Changing the terminology does not, of course, change the nature of the process by which some kinds of material are learned and most effectively taught. Nor does it alter the fact that conditioning procedures have been used by tyrants and would-be tyrants for evil purposes of indoctrination. But from this, it does not follow that a teacher who conditions a student to associate the letters c-a-t with the word *cat,* or who programs students to believe that all men are brothers, or that Paris is the capital of France, or that heroin is harmful, is acting as a tyrant, brain-washing, or producing mindless robots.

In short, whatever or however you end up feeling about conditioning as a means of teaching and learning is entirely up to you. All I ask at this point is that you keep an open mind and not be turned off by terminology.

BEHAVIOR MODIFICATION

The concept of education as behavior modification is based on the principle that most human behavior is learned. By the term *behavior*, I refer not only to a person's overt activities, but to her internal activities as well; not only to what she does physically, but also to what and how she feels, believes, thinks, perceives, values, etc. Except for a few simple reflex actions and innate drives or tendencies, all human behavior—including one's goals, tastes, skills, attitudes, etc.—are acquired and subject to modification.

The purpose of education has always been to change people in certain way—by teaching them, for example, to read, write, spell, and brush their teeth. A person who learns to drive a car or speak Italian or write his name is, in a sense, a changed person, somehow different after the learning experience than he had been before. This is really what behavior modification is all about.

The purpose of education, according to the behavior modification approach, is very simple and quite traditional: to teach students certain specific skills or ideas or other "new and better" ways of behaving, internally as well as externally, which will be to their advantage as individuals and to the advantage of the community in which they live. Thus, there is nothing revolutionary and certainly nothing insidious about the idea of behavior modification. The term can serve a useful purpose, however, if it helps us understand more clearly what learning is, how it takes place, and how it can be facilitated.

TEACHER BEHAVIOR

In Chapter 3 a distinction was made between two main kinds of student behaviors: desired and undesired. A distinction can also be made between two main kinds of teacher behavior. These correspond to the two main aspects of the teaching process.

The first has to do with eliciting the desired response from the student or eliminating his undesired responses. This involves formulating objectives, selecting, preparing, organizing and presenting material, planning lessons, showing, explaining, asking questions, and doing the other kinds of things that are ordinarily implied by the term *teaching*. From the standpoint of behavioral psychology, this aspect of the teacher's job has been referred to as programming or stimulus control. It implies the use of what were previously referred to as discriminative stimuli—words, pictures, books, models, films, and any other stimuli that seem to be capable of bringing about rather specific predetermined responses on the part of the students.

The second aspect of teaching is no less important than the first, but is frequently overlooked and is sometimes not thought of as part of the teaching process at all. This type of teacher behavior, reinforcement, involves responding in some way to what the student says or does or tries to do. It has to do with encouraging the student, providing him with feedback to let him know how he is progressing, correcting his errors or better yet helping him to correct them himself, and systematically rewarding him as he approximates the desired behavior in order to keep up his interest and his effort. This aspect of teaching centers around the use of reinforcing, rather than discriminative, stimuli and is sometimes referred to as contingency management. It is called by that name because the student's rewards (approval, etc.) are contingent (or dependent) upon his responding in a particular manner. The teacher manages the classroom situation in such a way that reinforcement is given or withheld depending upon what the student does or fails to do.

Teaching in this sense is a formal, deliberate, systematic attempt to get the student to do—or know or say or feel or believe—what she thinks he should. The assumption is that teachers are capable of deciding what it is that students should learn and how they should learn it. This, of course, is teaching in the conventional sense of giving, transmitting, conveying. Later in this chapter we shall discuss a rather different concept of teaching. But for now, let's continue with this more traditional view.

TEACHER-CENTERED CLASSROOMS

Behavioral psychology, association theories of learning, and the concept of learning-as-conditioning give strong support to so-called teacher centered classrooms. Such a classroom is one in which the teacher not only decides in advance what the students are to learn, but he plans, organizes and directs their work, selecting materials, giving assignments, presenting explanations, and doing whatever else he thinks necessary so that they will learn it. He tests them periodically to find out whether or to what extent they have learned the prescribed material; if they have not done so satisfactorily, he reteaches or provides the necessary remedial work. There is, of course, nothing very mysterious about teacher centered classrooms. These are conventional classrooms in the likes of which most of us have probably spent anywhere from 12 to 16 years or more. They are, however, rather different from the student centered classrooms, outgrowths of humanistic psychology, cognitive theories of learning, and the concept of learning as discovery, which are discussed later in this chapter.

The teacher, who is very much in charge of the situation, is an authority figure. The students' interests, desires, suggestions, etc. are likely to be taken into account, but they are not the final or the most decisive factors in determining what is to be learned, or how. This is not to suggest that such teachers are not interested in the individualization of instruction. Proponents of behavior modification and teaching through conditioning are very much interested in individualizing work. As we shall see in Chapter 10, a variety of procedures are employed in teacher centered classrooms as a means of providing for individual differences among students. But individualization of instruction in a teacher centered classroom is not a matter of permitting, much less encouraging, each child to go off in his own direction to do whatever he might happen to feel like doing at a given moment. Individualization is, rather, an attempt to help each student learn at his own rate, and possibly in his own way, material that has been prescribed as good or necessary for him.

ANALYSIS OF BEHAVIOR MODIFICATION

Before discussing the principles of behavior modification with reference to scholastic achievement, I think it would be helpful to consider how you can implement this strategy in the area of classroom management. The discipline problem, as has been suggested, can be thought of as essentially a matter of teaching students to make desired and avoid undesired responses. For our present purposes the process can be broken down into seven steps.

1. *Pinpoint the target behavior.* Identify as precisely as possible the particular disruptive acts or undesired responses that you would like to terminate. The more specific you can be in this respect the better. To say, for example, that little Cedric is hostile or uncooperative or hyperactive is not nearly specific enough. These terms are too vague and general to be of much use in a systematic attempt at changing Cedric's behavior. What specifically does little Cedric do that causes you to refer to him as hostile or uncooperative? Well, you say, he's "always" hitting other children, or talking out of turn, or getting up and leaving his seat. These, then, are your target behaviors. When there are several target behaviors, you are advised to single out and concentrate on the one that you find most disruptive or that you believe can be most readily modified.

2. *Specify the goal behavior.* This is the other side of the coin, so to speak, of the target behavior. Goal behavior refers to the desired responses you wish to bring out, the things you want little Cedric to do. Here again you should be as precise as possible. Instead of setting such fuzzy goals as getting Cedric to "act properly," or "behave himself," or to be "more attentive and cooperative," it is necessary in behavior modification to be more specific. You might, for example, want him to remain in his seat until given permission to leave. Other behaviors might be stated as follows:

> The students will
> have their work completed on time
> wait their turn at the drinking fountain
> keep their desks or work areas clean
> remain silent while another student or the teacher
> is speaking

These desired behaviors might constitute performance objectives, a concept that we shall discuss with respect to scholastic learning a little later in this chapter.

117

3. *Determine the frequency with which the target be-havior occurs.* Surely Cedric is not literally "always" fighting, or leaving his seat, or using obscene language. Maybe he does not do these things nearly as often as you think he does, or as often as some of his classmates do. In any event, behavior shapers strongly recommend that you ascertain and record the number of times a student acts in the undesired ways. By keeping a tally sheet on your desk and using time samples you might find, for example, that Cedric leaves his seat on the average of ten times a day. Now you have what is called a baseline against which to measure the effectiveness of your intervention program.

4. *Note the antecedents of the misbehavior.* It is not necessary, and might be impossible, for you to find the deeply-rooted psychological causes of Cedric's un-willingness to remain in his seat. But you can and should observe and record the circumstances or condi-tions under which he does so, and the events that were taking place immediately prior to his undesired be-havior. You might note, for example, that Cedric is most likely to leave his seat when you are talking to another student, or when your back is turned, or when little Griselda smiles at him. These events might be among the discriminative stimuli that elicit Cedric's particular response. Strictly speaking, the problem is not to try to find out why the student misbehaves but what hap-pened just before he misbehaved. You will need this information when you get to step 6.

5. *Identify the consequences of the behavior.* What happens to Cedric immediately after he leaves his seat? One of the basic principles of behavior modification is that Cedric's behavior is somehow reinforced. Perhaps he is rewarded by the full and undivided attention he receives from you, the teacher, as you momentarily ignore the rest of the class and concentrate on him, calling him by name, urging him to get back to his seat, telling him that you are not going to remind him again, and then a few minutes later reminding him that you are not going to remind him again. Perhaps it is the recognition and approval of his peers that he finds reinforcing. Perhaps it is the temporary relief to his aching posterior that serves as the reinforcer.

6. *Formulate and try out a hypothesis.* The five preceding steps are not merely preliminaries; they are essential parts of a total behavior modification program. But as is the case with other forms of problem solving, the formulation and testing of hypotheses is at the very heart of the process. Having identified the antecedents and the consequences of the desired and undesired behavior, you are now in a position to make a prediction, to plan and carry out a campaign.

   You hypothesize that if you do this, Cedric will do that. Then you do this and see whether Cedric does indeed do that. You might, for example, hypothesize that if you stand close to Cedric's desk as often as possible, he will not leave his seat so frequently. Other hypotheses might be that he will remain in his seat if you ignore him when he is out of his seat; or if you call him by name only when he is seated; or if you systematically register approval of other students who are properly seated; or if you can somehow get Griselda to stop looking at him; or if you smile at him after, say, every two minute interval that he is in his seat; or if you offer him some sort of reward for staying put.

   This step, of course, involves the use of the operant conditioning principles that were discussed in Chapter 3: varieties of positive reinforcers, negative reinforcement, punishment, extinction, schedules of reinforcement, etc. If you have forgotten about these concepts, it might be worth your while at this point to review them. Formulating hypotheses and implementing intervention programs also implies the use of some of the motivational strategies, such as tangible reinforcers and other incentives, that are discussed in Chapter 8.

7. *Check your results.* The final step is to determine the frequency of the target behavior after your plan has been in effect for a while and compare it with what it was initially. For example, in establishing your baseline in step 3, you found that Cedric left his seat without permission about ten times a day. After a few days of systematic intervention, you might find that his seat-leaving behavior has been reduced to, say, an average of five times a day. Your problem has not been completely solved, but you (and Cedric) have made some measurable progress. You have evidence that your strategy has

worked, or at least that you are on the right track. If the post-check shows no improvement in Cedric's behavior, you might have to formulate or try out another hypothesis, try to find more effective reinforcers, or try to control the discriminative stimuli that are interfering with your strategy.

As I hope you realize, the principles and techniques of behavior modification are by no means simple, nor are they guaranteed to bring about the desired results in each and every case. In these few pages and in Chapter 3 I have only touched upon some of the more important of these principles and techniques. For further enlightenment along these lines, I should like to refer you to some of the books mentioned in the bibliographies that deal with this subject exclusively. Next, let us see how these principles are related to scholastic learning.

PERFORMANCE OBJECTIVES

A teacher, you will recall, can be thought of as a kind of behavioral engineer. Just about every engineer needs, among other things, a blueprint or a plan or a model of what his finished product will be like. He cannot settle for a vague, fuzzy, general notion of what his bridge, for example, will look like or be able to do. He needs a clear, specific, detailed picture of the bridge as it will be when completed. The teacher's equivalent of the bridge is the student. His equivalent of the engineer's blueprint is the lesson plan. One of the most important parts of a good lesson plan is the statement of objectives. If the teacher does not have a clear, preconceived idea of the product he would like to produce, it is not likely that he will be successful in producing it.

Objectives are sometimes stated very loosely, in vague, ambiguous terms such as the following:

To educate the whole child.
To help the person fulfill himself as an individual.
To prepare him for good citizenship.

120

To develop an appreciation of literature.
To foster personality adjustment.
To promote creativity or independent thinking.
To teach the child how to read.
To bring about an understanding of biology.

Some teachers indicate that their objective is to bring about a *real* understanding of their subject, as though emphasizing the word *real* made any difference.

Objectives stated in terms such as these have a beautiful ring to them. They certainly represent lofty ideals, and in a general way they are certainly worth aiming at. But perhaps they are too general, too vague, too ambiguous, too abstract to be of much use to the teacher or the student or anyone else.

What, for example, do we mean by "fulfilling oneself as an individual"? How or where do we begin to educate a "whole child"? What does a person who "appreciates literature" do to indicate that he does indeed appreciate it? How can you tell whether a student understands (or really understands) biology? What are the specific skills that a child must master before it can be fairly said that he knows how to read?

Ambiguously stated objectives such as those mentioned above give the teacher no sense of direction, no idea of where to begin or how to proceed. They give the student no clear idea of what he is expected to learn or how he is expected to learn it. There is no way of determining whether or to what extent objectives such as these have been attained or whether any progress toward their attainment has been made. Far more useful—at least in some cases—are so called performance, or behavioral, objectives.

A performance objective is a clear, specific statement of what we have previously referred to as the desired behavior. It is a precise description of what the student will be able to do as a consequence of the instruction he receives. It is stated in terms of behavior that can be observed and measured so that there is some objective way of determining the extent to which it has been achieved. Performance objectives might not be feasible, or even desirable, in all subject areas. But they are especially recommended for so-called content subjects where there is rather specific material that students are expected to master.

121

FORMULATING PERFORMANCE OBJECTIVES

Performance objectives include four elements: subject, verb, conditions, and standards.

Performance objectives are stated in the form of a complete sentence (not just a phrase). Like any other sentence, they must have a subject. The subject of a performance objective is always the student. It is not a statement of what the teacher will do or what the course will cover. It is, rather, a description or a prediction of what the student will do.

In planning your lessons or writing out your objectives, you might do well to begin as follows:

At the end of this class (or week or unit or term), the student will be able to do the following:

1.

2.

3.

Next comes the second and most critical element, the verb. The verb specifies as clearly as possible what the student will be able to do. Here you are urged to avoid such ambiguous words as know, understand, appreciate, and comprehend. Instead, you should use such specific action verbs as name, list, explain, define, identify, summarize, and compare.

Such action verbs, you will recognize, are of the type likely to be used on tests. This is no mere coincidence. Proponents of performance objectives maintain that the very same verbs used in the statement of objectives should be used in the corresponding tests to determine whether they have been attained. This ties in with the idea that course or unit objectives should not be kept secret, but that students should be informed in advance what it is that they are expected to learn, and what it is that they will be expected to do in order to demonstrate that they have learned it. Using educational psychology as an example:

At the end of this unit, the student will be able to:

1. Identify Ivan Pavlov.

2. Explain how concepts are formed.

3. Compare teacher-centered with student-centered classrooms.

4. List the four main elements of performance objectives.

Presumably, students who are informed in advance that these are the kinds of behaviors they will be expected to perform (or responses they will be asked to make) can and will study more efficiently than would be the case if they were simply told to "know" or "understand" or "really understand" educational psychology.

The third element in a performance objective has to do with the conditions under which the student will be expected to make the desired response. These usually refer to the testing conditions and might be well enough understood so that they need not be made explicit. The following are some examples of conditions that should be made explicit:

In 100 words or less, the student will summarize the plot of *Catcher in the Rye.*

Given 25 English nouns (from a specified list), the student will, using a dictionary if he wishes, provide the French equivalent.

Without the use of notes, textbooks, or other reference materials, the student will describe in chronological order four events that led to the Declaration of Independence.

Given a list of 20 statements about World World War II, the student will indicate whether each is true or false.

The fourth and final element of a performance objective indicates the quantity and the quality of the work expected. For example:

The student will type 40 words per minute with no more than one error per minute.

The student will spell correctly at least 80% of the words on a given list.

PRECISION TEACHING

After he has selected and carefully stated the objectives for a unit of instruction, the teacher's next task is to plan his strategies, that is, to devise effective means of eliciting the desired responses from his students. This, of course, involves choosing and adapting methods and materials that are likely to be the most productive for those particular purposes in that particular classroom situation. The method of instruction most closely identified with the concept of learning-as-conditioning is commonly referred to as *programming*. But to avoid the mechanistic connotations of the word programming, the term precision teaching is sometimes used to designate this type of methodology.

In precision teaching, the material to be learned (e.g., psychology) is broken down into units(e.g., behavioral psychology). These units are then divided into what might be called subunits (e.g., classical conditioning) which are subdivided into still smaller segments or modules (e.g., who Pavlov was, when and where he lived, and what he did). These segments, which correspond to the performance objectives, are presented to the students systematically in small sequential steps. Usually the teacher begins with the simplest or most basic concepts and progresses toward those which are more complex. The student is expected to respond to each of these presentations by doing something to indicate that he has learned them. Ideally, each of his responses, be they written or spoken or manual, is immediately and positively reinforced.

The material to be learned is organized and presented in such a way—bit by small bit, step by small step, with many cues, frequent repetition, and a great deal of reinforcement—that the student is all but certain to make the desired response. With this systematic feedback, regular encouragement, and almost constant direction, the student masters one idea or principle or whatever before proceeding to the next. In this way, mastery of each little segment is practically assured.

TEACHING MACHINES

The method of instruction that has just been described underlies the use of teaching machines, computers, programmed textbooks and other so-called auto-instructional devices. While programming does sometimes involve the use of mechanical or electronic equipment, it need not do so.

In the later 1950s, B.F. Skinner set forth his now well-known claim that one of the most serious shortcomings of the typical traditional classroom is the relative infrequency of reinforcement and the long time lapse between the reinforcement and the behavior with which it is intended to be associated. For optimum learning to take place, he believes, immediate positive reinforcement should follow each step of the learning process. He notes, moreover, that in conventional classroom recitations, only a few students make only a few responses, while the majority remain passive and do nothing to warrant reinforcement. To remedy this stiuation, he devised and strongly recommends the use of automated teaching machines.

Teaching machines have not revolutionized education, as some educational prophets of the 1950s had predicted, but they have had an impact. Most of the behaviorists that I have ever heard of do not believe for a moment that machines can or ever will replace human teachers. Rather, they regard machines as potentially useful tools—in a class with visual aids—but hardly indispensable. Programming, or precision teaching if you prefer, is not, therefore, a technological product of the electronic age. It is a refinement of what well-organized teachers have been doing for centuries.

FACILITATING DISCOVERY

While programming might well be the more efficient way of teaching students to master specific, predetermined content, there are subject areas and fields within particular content areas where a discovery approach might be more appropriate. Programming and discovery methods of teaching are not mutually exclusive, and neither has been proved to be better than the other in general. In the course of a day, many teachers are likely to use some of each or a combination of the two. Discovery methods, you will recall, correspond to cognitive theories of learning and humanistic systems of psychology. Having noted some of the behavioristic principles and assumptions that underlie programming, let us at

this point review some of the humanistic assumptions that underlie discovery methods and the related concept of student centered
classrooms.

ASSUMPTIONS

One of the key assumptions underlying cognitive theories of learning is that individuals behave in accordance with the manner in
which they perceive their environments. A basic principle of
learning that follows from this assumption is that knowledge,
skills, attitudes, values, etc., are most likely to affect a person, or
have meaning for her, when and if she finds them out by and for
herself, and when they are perceived as being related to the satisfaction of her needs or the attainment of her goals.

Learning, according to the humanists, is a natural process
that does not have to be, and should not be, forced or artificially
stimulated. Children, of course, do not always want to learn what
their teachers want them to learn, nor do they necessarily want to
learn in the way their teachers might prefer. When such is the
case, humanists see little value, but many disadvantages, in forcing
them. What distresses many humanists is the preoccupation of the
educational system with requiring students to learn things they do
not particularly want to learn and see no value in learning, instead
of helping them learn the kinds of things they do want to learn
and feel that they need to learn for their own self-fulfillment.

If a child perceives the meaning of the material he is expected to learn, if he sees how it will help him become the kind of
person he wants to become, he will want to learn it and he will
learn it. Otherwise, he will have to be "extrinsically motivated"
by some artificial system of rewards and punishment. Better,
humanists maintain, to let learning occur "naturally," insofar as
possible, with a minimum of external intervention.

Cognitive theorists, by and large, believe that schools should
capitalize on, rather than suppress and frustrate, students' natural
tendencies to explore, to manipulate their environment, to experiment, to inquire, to guess, to take the initiative, and to act independently. Teachers, they believe, should devise and employ
ways and means of helping the individual student come to perceive

learning as a means of attaining his goals rather than goals that have been set for him by the school administration.

Toward this end, the school should provide opportunities for the student to come to think of himself as a responsible, contributing member of a democratic society. The classroom should be a place where the student not only learns "content," but where he can and will develop a favorable self-concept and a feeling of personal worth. He should be given sufficient freedom to help plan his own educational program and should have ample opportunities for experiencing success and a feeling of accomplishment with respect to activities that he himself considers worthwhile. For purposes such as these, and to help students learn "how to learn," humanistic educators are inclined to favor a so-called student centered classroom over one which is more teacher centered.

STUDENT-CENTERED CLASSES

Contrary to what is sometimes thought, the kind of student centered classroom favored by humanists is not one in which students are permitted, much less encouraged, to run wild, each doing whatever he happens to feel like doing at a given moment. But neither is it a setting in which the teacher is regarded as omniscient, nor does he make all of the decisions.

In a student centered classroom, more emphasis is placed on the existing interests, problems, and needs of the individual student. There is more in the way of cooperative teacher-student planning, personal involvement, and social interaction. While the students do not have all the say, or make the final determination about what will be learned and how, their voice is heard and their desires respected.

One of the main functions of the teacher in this arrangement is to try to relate the material to be learned to the needs of the individual student; to help him see the relevance of that material to his own life; and to make it fit his life style or frame of reference, rather than vice versa. In a student centered classroom there is more of an effort to develop the student's initiative and sense of personal responsibility for his own education, as well as his powers of creativity and self-expression. The teacher, in

127

short, is not so much concerned with bringing about predetermined "desired responses" as he is with trying to help the student develop new insights which will be meaningful to her at her stage of development.

The teacher might well be convinced that there are certain things that the student should learn because he will need them two or three or ten years in the future. The student, however, is likely to be much more concerned with the here and now. Therefore, the teacher who is familiar with cognitive theories of learning and wants to implement them will try to perceive the student's present situation (her interests, her problems, her aspirations, etc.) as she does, so that he can make that important material more meaningful to her in her present situation.

Instead of using the principle of "logical organization" of material, which corresponds to programming methods of teaching, the teacher in a student centered classroom, using a discovery approach, is likely to use "psychological organization." What is or seems logical to a teacher is not always logical to the student. One who knows a given field rather well can ordinarily perceive logical relationships that are not nearly so apparent to one who is just beginning to investigate that field. A social studies teacher, for example, might be convinced that it is logical to study the historical background of a contemporary problem before dealing with the problem itself. To a student, however, it might seem to make a lot more sense to begin with the current problem and work backward, picking up the historical background when and as it is needed.

To a teacher, it might seem most illogical to try to teach point D in her outline without first having "covered" points A, B, and C, or to skip from B to G and then back to C. But to the student, who at the moment is very much interested in G and could not care less about C through F, her logic might not be his. Certain subjects which are cumulative in nature may have to be taught in logical, sequential order. But the principle of psychological organization focuses on the student rather than the subject matter. Although the teacher does have an outline or a lesson plan to guide her when using this principle, she is ready and willing to depart from it, or modify it, in order to capitalize on her students' curiosity or present concerns.

OBJECTIVES

From what has just been said, it might be apparent that proponents of student centered classrooms and discovery methods of teaching are not overly enthusiastic about performance objectives. Having recommended such objectives for those kinds of classes in which students are expected to master (or at least learn rather thoroughly) a prescribed body of knowledge or a specified set of skills, I must now hasten to point out that there are other courses or subject areas or units of instruction where they might not be nearly as appropriate. This is particularly the case with regard to affective outcomes involving such subjective, emotionally toned responses as feeling, believing, accepting, appreciating, preferring, valuing, and the like.

Such "desired responses" might be difficult, if not impossible, to reduce to observable, measurable behavior. It does not follow, therefore, that they should be discarded as desirable educational goals. It might be difficult, for example, to fit something like "appreciation of literature" into the standard performance objective format which was described a few pages back. It would be a mistake, however, to conclude that students cannot be guided toward an appreciation of literature or that teachers should not even attempt to so guide them. Certain affective outcomes, in short, might not lend themselves to programming (with the implication of specific objectives) as well as they do to a discovery approach (which often implies goals that are admittedly vague and difficult to define behaviorally.)

Even cognitive objectives are not always best stated in terms of specific student behavior. When an attempt is made to do so, there is always the possibility that the result might be little more than a collection of disorganized, unrelated bits of information. A teacher who is interested in helping her students perceive the basic structure of a subject, derive personal meaning from that subject, recognize the complex interrelationships within a subject, might have difficulty with the whole concept of performance objectives. So is one who is concerned with guiding her students toward a broad overview of a subject, and would like them to discover relationships and generalizations for themselves. There is no good reason why such teachers should have to use performance objectives. For their purposes, broad, general, and even vague objectives might be considerably more appropriate.

DISCOVERY METHODS OF TEACHING

Cognitive theories of learning do not yield the neat, precise, detailed, step-by-step methodology that results from association theories. In fact, one of the chief criticisms of cognitive theories centers around this very point: that, unlike association theories, they do not tell the teacher specifically what to do and how to do it. Admittedly, there is no set formula for facilitating discovery as there is for programming. There are no predetermined steps that a teacher must take, no particular sequence that he must follow, no rules or fixed pattern of behavior to which he must conform. Nor can there be because, in a sense, the whole point of discovery learning is spontaneity, flexibility, adaptability, informality, etc.

The distinguishing characteristic of discovery methods of teaching is that insofar as possible the teacher organizes and conducts her class so that the student can and will learn through his own activities with a minimum of teacher intervention. The student is encouraged and expected to rely, not entirely, of course, but to a great extent, on his own experience, observations, and independent thinking. The classroom situation is structured so that he is challenged and encouraged to follow his curiosity by asking appropriate questions and formulating his own tentative answers. The quality of his questions is likely to be considered more important than that of his answers.

The purpose of discovery methods, as we have seen, is not to transmit to the student prepackaged bodies of knowledge that someone else has organized. It is, rather, to enable the student to participate as fully as possible in the process of knowledge-acquisition. The emphasis is not so much on the product or the outcome of the learning experience as it is on the process of learning itself. For example, instead of simply informing her students of a particular scientific principle, the teacher might guide her students through the process that the scientist himself went through in discovering that principle. She might attempt to have them ask the kinds of questions he asked, see the relationships that he saw as he saw them, experiment somewhat as he experimented, maybe even feel frustrated at times as he did, and experience the joy of success, the joy of discovery, somewhat as he did.

To cite a couple of other examples, instead of simply giving students the spelling rule about *i before e except after c*, etc., a teacher might present a variety of words that include *ie* and *ei* combinations and help them arrive at that rule inductively. Having discovered that rule for themselves, the teacher can then arrange for them to discover the part about "when sounded as *a* as in neighbor and weigh." Or instead of informing them of the formula for finding the area of a rectangle, she might provide them with appropriate materials such as one-inch-square cards which they can arrange in patterns of various lengths and widths, counting and measuring as they go along, until they eventually discover the formula for themselves.

Methods of teaching based on imitation rather than trial and error, on giving information, presenting material, telling students and explaining things to them simply and directly are likely to be quicker and more efficient than time-consuming discovery methods. Besides, a student might "discover" a "wrong answer." For reasons such as these, very few if any responsible educators maintain that everything should be learned through personal discovery or that all subjects should be taught in this way. There are, however, opportunities for teachers in just about every subject area at every grade level to use a discovery approach occasionally, just as there are likely to be occasions when programming would be far more effective.

Since there is no prescription for discovery (or, as it is frequently called, inquiry) teaching, each teacher has to discover for himself when and how best to employ this approach. Actually, the discovery "method" is not so much a matter of technique as it is an attitude on the part of the teacher: an attitude toward students and toward the learning process brought out in the section above headed "Assumptions." It is, in other words, not so much a matter of following a predetermined plan with a specific set of objectives or desired responses, although it can be used in connection with programming. Recall, for example, the method of learning the spelling rule that was just given.

Essentially, discovery methods imply providing facilities and encouragement, challenges and opportunities, for the individual to find out for himself, or think for himself, and an atmosphere of freedom and support that is conducive to independent thinking.

TEACHING FOR THINKING

Chapter 5, you may recall, centers around several so-called modes of thinking: convergent and divergent thinking, inductive and deductive reasoning, critical and creative thinking, intuition, reflection, and problem solving. Each of these, you will recognize, is a potential means of learning by discovery. For the remainder of this chapter we shall focus on the role of the teacher in guiding the thinking aspects of learning. Since the various modes of thinking overlap considerably, as we have seen, instead of dealing with each separately, let's consider them together.

THINKING AS AN ART

Thinking is an art that has a great deal in common with other arts. For example, like other arts, thinking requires a certain talent, or aptitude, or kind of intelligence. Not everyone has the ability to become an outstanding thinker any more than he has what it takes to become an outstanding musician or athlete. Most people do have the aptitude for good thinking, but they do not always use it. One very important function of education, therefore, is to develop a person's thinking abilities and help him learn how to use them.

Like other arts, good thinking can be learned informally, independently, without formal instruction. Just as some people, especially those with a great deal of native ability, learn to play the piano quite well without ever having had a lesson in their lives, so are there those who have learned to do good, clear thinking pretty much on their own. Nevertheless, the assumption underlying schools (or piano lessons) is that they can be made to help.

Like other arts, thinking presumes a great many skills and

sub-skills. Let's take baseball playing as an analogy. To play baseball well, a person must be able to catch a ball. He must be able to catch ground balls, pop flies, line drives, and high flies. He must be able to hit fastballs, curves, and maybe even knuckleballs. He must be able to throw, run, slide, etc. He must also, of course, know the rules and understand some of the strategy of the game. To teach a person how to play baseball, therefore, it is necessary to have a rather specific idea of what it is that good players are able to do. To improve his performance as a player, it is necessary to identify those particular skills in which he needs special help so that his coach can provide the necessary instruction and practice.

If you do not consider baseball playing to be an art, use piano playing, cooking, sculpting, gardening or some other art as an example instead. All of these are so complex that they cannot be taught, or developed, or learned all at once. They must be broken down into component parts or sub-skills. Much the same is true of, say, problem solving.

THINKING OBJECTIVES

While it is not as easy to identify the particular behaviors of problem solving as it is those of baseball playing, the principle is the same. A good problem solver, for example, is able to recognize and define problems, gather and organize data, make logical deductions, draw inferences inductively, weigh evidence, distinguish fact from opinion, recognize and avoid fallacies, etc.

These behaviors might well be used as performance objectives of a course or unit intended to improve the quality of students' thinking. As you may recall from our discussion of performance objectives earlier in this chapter, objectives stated in terms of teaching students "how to think" or "how to solve problems" might be too broad, vague, and abstract to be attainable or even useful. But by breaking the process down into smaller, more specific skills, we can identify a number of "desired responses" that can be taught in practically any subject matter area.

133

PRACTICE

Like other arts, thinking is learned mainly by doing. To become proficient in this art, one requires a great deal of practice. As we saw in Chapter 2, however, unguided, undirected practice alone is not likely to prove very effective. As is the case in the learning of other skills, the student needs someone to model the desired behavior, to point out his errors or weaknesses and to make suggestions for overcoming them. The learner needs someone to explain or demonstrate how he can improve his performance. He needs encouragement and support and someone to keep him informed of his progress. In short, he needs coaching, along with practice, in learning the art of thinking as he does in learning any other art.

Thinking, as we have been using that term, is not simply a spontaneous expression of one's transitory feelings about a matter. It is, rather, a kind of mental activity that requires, among other things, a great deal of preparation, a store of information on which to draw, and a lot of intellectual discipline. Practicing the art of thinking, therefore, requires something more than engaging in what have been called bull or rap sessions. Discussions, of course, can be extremely valuable means of providing the kind of practice under consideration—provided they include the conditions and the guidance or direction referred to above.

As a means of providing students with opportunities to improve the quality of their thinking, it is not enough to ask them what they think, listen to their off-the-top-of-their-heads opinion, and let it go at that. Nor is it enough for a teacher to simply exhort his students to think, or to hang up a sign on the bulletin board with the word "Think" followed by an exclamation point printed in big bold letters.

Teachers who are genuinely interested in improving their students' thinking can and should give them assignments that require them to practice the kinds of behavior specified in their list of objectives: to make logical deductions, draw inferences inductively, gather and organize data from a variety of sources, compare different points of view, formulate and test hypotheses, etc.

Whether it is in connection with a discussion, a homework assignment, individual seat work, ordinary classroom recitations, projects or whatever, the teacher must have a clear notion of what she wants her students to do; she must challenge them and give them an opportunity to practice doing these things; and she must help them do those things better. This is what teaching for thinking, or teaching anything else, is really all about.

SUGGESTIONS FOR TEACHERS

In Chapter 2 we observed that a number of behaviors associated with independent thinking can be modeled by teachers and that these consequently might be imitated by students. At this point, you might wish to review that section. In addition to modeling, there are many other things you can do as a teacher to help your students learn to think more effectively.

You can begin, for example, by giving them something to think about. You can stimulate their thinking by structuring the learning situation so that genuine problems emerge. You can guide them toward an awareness of unanswered questions and unresolved difficulties in your subject area. You can create doubts in their minds. You can challenge their existing beliefs. You can show them when and how their opinions are inconsistent. You can bring other viewpoints to their attention. You can help them perceive the implications of their position and the assumptions on which it is based. You will not, I hope, be satisfied to simply stir up problems or confuse the student about his existing views, and then leave him entirely to his own devices to straighten things out for himself. You will, I presume, want to help him reach valid, responsible conclusions that are, nevertheless, his.

Toward this end, you can invite your students to ask questions, but you need not be in a hurry to answer them. Perhaps by skillfully asking questions of your own in an appropriate sequence you can draw the answer out of the student himself. You can not only permit but actively encourage your students to express their doubts, to demand proof, and to refuse to accept everything you say on your word alone. You can go out of your way to make sure that you do not in any way penalize them for expressing views different from your own or from those of the textbook. In encouraging your students to set forth their own opinions, you can help them understand that is their responsibility to defend those opinions against objections that you or other students might raise. All of these things, of course, should be done in a supportive classroom atmosphere where students and teacher respect one another's views without necessarily accepting them.

Please note that in this chapter, as well as in Chapter 5, we have been considering thinking as a highly desirable end in itself as well as a tremendously important means toward further learning. Thus, learning how to think is essentially a matter of learning how to discover, or of learning how to learn.

In conclusion, please remember that in order to think, we must think about something. In order to think about that something, we must know something about it. We need facts, knowledge, data, or information to think about. Thus, one indispensable element in "teaching for thinking" is to see to it that your students have this necessary knowledge at their disposal. If you judge programming to be the most effective means of helping them acquire and retain this knowledge, use programming. If you believe that your students are more likely to acquire and retain and be able to apply this necessary information through some sort of discovery approach, use some sort of discovery approach. But do not make the mistake that some teachers make in believing that they can do very much to help their students think clearly and independently without first going through the process of learning in the more restricted sense of acquiring knowledge.

SUMMARY

Just above everyone agrees on the need for good teachers, but there is no general agreement as to precisely what it is that a good teacher does that distinguishes him or her from one who is not so good. Neither is there any one method of teaching that in and of itself is always or necessarily better than others.

One approach to teaching is programming, or behavior modification, or precision teaching, all of which amount to essentially the same thing. Based on the concept of learning through conditioning, particularly operant conditioning, this type of strategy implies a systematic attempt on the part of a teacher to help students achieve rather specific predetermined outcomes.

Among the distinguishing features of precision teaching are the use of performance objectives, the presentation of material in small, sequential segments, and frequent reinforcement.

While precision teaching might well be the most efficient way of teaching students to master specific, predetermined content, there are other subject areas where a discovery approach might be more appropriate. There is no formula for discovery teaching as there is for programming, but the distinguishing characteristic of this strategy is that, insofar as possible, the teacher organizes and conducts his classes in such a way that students are helped and encouraged to learn through their own activities. Flexibility, spontaneity, informality, and student self-direction are likely to be among the other features of a class that is discovery oriented.

Closely related to discovery are methods of teaching intended to improve the quality of students' thinking. However, certain principles of precision teaching, such as the use of performance objectives, practice, and reinforcement, can also be used for this purpose. In order to think critically or to solve problems, we need data to think about, or ideas to reorganize. Either programming or discovery or some combination of these two kinds of strategies can be used to help students acquire the knowledge they will need in order to think more clearly and productively.

Few, if any, teachers rely solely or exclusively on programming or discovery methods of teaching. A teacher's task is not to decide which of these strategies is the best in general, but which to use at this particular time with these particular students for this particular purpose.

Recommended Readings

Becker, Wesley C. et al. *Teaching 2: Cognitive Learning and Instruction.* Chicago: Science Research Associates, 1975. A partially-programmed book intended for self-paced instruction, similar to *Teaching 1,* which was recommended in the reading list for Chapter 3. This volume includes an operant conditioning model for the teaching of concepts and problem solving behavior, as well as a comparison of Piaget's cognitive-development theory with behaviorism.

Dunkin, M.J., and Biddle, B.J. *The Study of Teaching.* New York: Holt, Rinehart and Winston, 1974. The most comprehensive summary to date of research on teacher effectiveness. Relates teacher behaviors to student achievement and attitudes.

Gage, N.L., and Berliner, D.C. *Educational Psychology.* Chicago: Rand McNally, 1975. Section G (units 21–30) of this comprehensive textbook treats in some detail the psychological bases of, and means of improving, various methodologies, including lecturing and explaining, discussions, individualized instruction, and teacher-student interaction.

Gilstrap, R.L., and Martin, W.R. *Current Strategies for Teachers.* Pacific Palisades, Cal.: Goodyear, 1975. Designed to help teachers individualize instruction. Among the strategies considered are lectures, discussion, drill and practice, discovery, simulation, independent study, and performance-based learning packages.

Good, Thomas L. et al. *Teachers Make a Difference.* New York: Holt, Rinehart, and Winston, 1975. A reply to those critics of education who

138

maintain that teachers do not make a great deal of difference. Includes a good review of research on teacher effectiveness, and informative chapters on accountability, criterion-referenced testing, and the goals of education.

Komaki, Judi. "Neglected Reinforcers in the College Classroom." *Journal of Higher Education.* Jan./Feb., 1975. Report of an experimental study involving the principles of reinforcement and something similar to the token economy at the college level. The author recommends that these principles be used more widely at that level.

Proefriedt, William A. *The Teacher You Choose to Be.* New York: Holt, Rinehart and Winston, 1975. A very interesting, timely, and readable book. Stresses the need for teachers to help students develop the critical capacities necessary for them to make their own intelligent value judgments.

Raths, Louis E. et al. *Teaching for Thinking.* Columbus, Ohio: Charles E. Merrill, 1966. Includes many practical suggestions for use at the elementary and high school levels.

7

Retention and Application of Learning

One of the many definitions of learning is that it is the process by which knowledge, skills, values, etc., are acquired, retained, and applied. Like other definitions of learning, this one is far from being completely satisfactory. It is not universally accepted, nor is it beyond criticism. But it does serve a useful purpose. So far, we have been mainly concerned with the acquisition aspect of learning. In this chapter, we will consider the other two.

REMEMBERING AND FORGETTING

We can talk about learning and retention apart from one another, but actually these are not two separate and distinct processes. Rather, one implies the other. If you do not retain something for at least a very short time after you have been exposed to it, it

141

cannot be fairly said that you have learned it. Similarly, if you had never learned anything about a particular subject, you could hardly be expected to remember it. If learning, as has been suggested, can be thought of as a change in behavior, retention has to do with the duration of that change.

Many of the things you experienced years ago, or maybe even a few minutes ago, you have already forgotten. Maybe in some cases it is just as well that you did. Some of the things you have forgotten were frankly not worth remembering. All of us have acquired certain bits of information (such as the latest football scores) which might have been important to us for a short period of time, but then ceased to serve any useful purpose. Our having forgotten them is certainly no great loss. Perhaps those bits of information dealt with situations that no longer exist (such as the address of a friend who has since moved) or they have been superseded by more recent or more significant information (such as the friend's current address.)

Just as it would be a big waste if we promptly forgot everything we learned, so would it be rather useless for us to remember, or even try to remember, everything that we at one time knew. There are some experiences which, as we say, we'll "never forget" or "can't forget." But there are others which we would "just as soon forget" or "try not to remember." And then there are those things we would like to remember—at least until next Friday's quiz—but have difficulty in remembering and which require a special effort on our part to retain.

Despite the tendencies on the part of some teachers and pseudo-sophisticated students to disparage "mere memory," most teachers want and expect their students to remember some of the more important material they are taught long beyond next Friday's quiz. They recognize that without information which has been "stored" in the memory, such so-called higher mental processes as problem solving and critical thinking are practically impossible. While there is undeniably a lot more to learning than memorizing, remembering is an indispensable element in the total learning process.

MEMORY

A useful distinction is commonly made between two forms of memory; rote and logical. Like the majority of other educators, we'll be particularly concerned with the latter, but let's see how the two are related.

Rote memory refers to what used to be called (and perhaps in some circles still is) learning "by heart." This involves the retention of material so that it can be repeated verbatim, even though it might not be understood. Rote memorization can be readily explained in terms of imitation or simple conditioning. It represents what is usually thought of as one of the lowest or simplest ways of learning. While rote memorization is not the only way, and not necessarily the best way, it is one way of remembering certain facts, definitions, formulas, and other bits of information, especially when precision or having exactly the right words is at a premium.

Logical memory is the retention of material through a network of meaningful associations. It presumes understanding. It involves the organization of ideas and the perception of relationships among them so that we remember the structure or the general outline of a subject even though some of the details are forgotten. By means of rote memory a person might be able to recite a particular poem, for example, without knowing what the words mean. Through logical memory, he might be able to paraphrase the poem and bring out its main points without necessarily remembering the author's exact words.

Rote memory, as well as the infinitely more complex process of logical memory, has a physical basis in a person's brain. But no one knows for sure what the exact nature of that electrochemical basis is or how it works. There is reason to believe that memory depends to a great extent on the presence in the brain of ribonucleic acid—RNA for short. But why or how this so-called memory molecule affects retention remains something of a mystery.

Research in this area has given rise to speculation about the possibility of "memory pills" or injections to help us retain more information for longer periods of time with little or no effort on our part. Such chemical aids have been used successfully with animals under laboratory conditons but they are not, of course, as yet available at your local drug store. A great deal of work remains to be done before they are, or before the workings of the brain with respect to memory are anywhere near being fully understood.

Whatever its physiological or neurological basis might be, memory is generally considered to be one of the "factors" or components of what has been called general intelligence. Just as individuals differ from one another in their verbal abilities, numerical abilities, abstract reasoning abilities, and overall IQ, so do they differ with respect to their memory abilities. A person who has a great deal of numerical or verbal ability, for example, might have a memory like the proverbial sieve, while one with a very good memory could be just average or even below average in general intelligence, reasoning ability, or in some of the other factors of intelligence.

So far I have been speaking of memory as though it were a single ability, but it is not. With respect to either rote or logical memory, a person who has a good memory for verbal material does not necessarily have as good a memory for, say, numbers or spatial designs. The ability to memorize a poem, for example, is not the same as the ability required for remembering telephone numbers, historical dates, mathematical facts, sketches, designs, or names and faces. More than the individual's interests are involved in these differential kinds of memory. Different kinds of mental abilities seem to be required.

In Chapter 9 we shall examine the concepts of general intelligence, learning abilities and disabilities more closely. As we shall see then, "intelligence" as well as memory and the other kinds of mental abilities that constitute "intelligence" are partially determined by heredity. To some extent, therefore, it is true that some people are "born with" better, or different kinds of, memories than others. But one of the purposes of education is to help the individual develop and use to the fullest extent possible the abilities, including memory, with which he has been endowed, however great or small they might be.

STORAGE AND RETRIEVAL

The term memory or retention implies not only the storage of information or experience, but also some system of retrieving that information or experience when it is needed. There are three main means of retrieving, or attempting to retrieve, information that has been stored in our memory cells. These three ways (recall, recognition, and relearning) correspond to the three main methods of measuring retention and forgetting in classrooms and in psychological laboratories. Thus, the answers to the questions, How much do we remember? or How rapidly do we forget? depend not only on whether we are referring to rote or logical memory, but also on the method of measuring retention and retrieval that is being employed.

Suppose, for example, that you are attending a reunion of your first grade class. Suppose that there were 20 other children in that class and that when you were in the first grade you knew all of their names. Suppose that now you can only associate 10 names with the appropriate faces. Through this "recall" method, which involves no prompting, it could be said that you had remembered (or forgotten) half of the material you once knew. Recall, of course, is the method of measuring retention used on completion type tests (the author of *The Pickwick Papers* was _____) and some essay tests (describe four of the leading characters in the *Pickwick Papers*).

At your first grade reunion, you would probably meet at least one person whose name you could not recall, but you would immediately recognize it if you heard it. "Oh, of course, Pete Koslowski. It was right on the tip of my tongue. . . ." If you were able to recall only 50% of the names, perhaps you could recognize an additional 25% of them for a total of 75%. Recognition, of course, is the means of measuring retrieval used in multiple choice and true-false tests. It is not likely that you would be given such a test at your class reunion, but if you were, you would undoubtedly score higher than you would on a test of recall. This, at least, is what usually happens in classroom test situations.

The "relearning" (or conservation) method of measuring retention is rarely used in classrooms. If it were, most of us would receive much higher grades than we do with either recall or recognition methods. This system is more likely to be used in psychological laboratories. The experimenter measures the amount of time (or number of trials) required for the initial learning. Then he compares it with the amount of time (or number of trials) required to learn it again later. The difference represents the amount that has been retained.

Suppose that it took a stranger (say the spouse of one of your classmates) 10 minutes (or 10 introductions) to learn the 20 names. Suppose that a year later, at the next annual reunion, it

145

took him only two minutes (or two trials) to "relearn" the same names. In this situation, since the relearning took only two-tenths of the time (or effort) needed for the original learning, it could be said that he had "saved," or retained, 80% of the material.

Perhaps at one time you had a rather large speaking vocabulary in a foreign language. Perhaps you have not used that language in a number of years and have forgotten, or think you have forgotten, many of the words that you formerly knew. If you now attempted to relearn that vocabulary you might be surprised to discover that more of it than you thought had been stored in your memory. Because of the phenomenon of conservation and the relative ease of relearning compared with initial learning or with either recall or recognition systems of retrieval, there are those who maintain that nothing that a person experiences is ever totally or completely forgotten. But surely some forgetting takes place, so the next questions are why and how.

INTERFERENCE

Forgetting is sometimes thought of as a passive process, a consequence of not using the material for an extended period of time. This is the simplest, but not the only, explanation of forgetting. For many years it was thought that forgetting is due to disintegration of neurological connections or deterioration of memory traces within the brain. Another explanation is that forgetting is an active process, the consequence of interference between earlier and subsequent learning. This interference takes two forms, depending upon its direction.

The interference of later learning with earlier learning is called retroactive inhibition. The interference works backwards, retroactively. In learning the names of people at a large social gathering, for example, you would perhaps have no difficulty in remembering the name of the first person you met if he were the only one to whom you were introduced that day. But then you meet a number of people and unless the first made a very great impression on you, chances are that by the time you meet the fifth or tenth new person, you will have forgotten the name of the first, as well as the second, third, etc. Thus, learning new material actually caused you to forget material you had learned earlier.

Similarly, in a classroom situation, concepts, theories, principles, facts, etc., learned today can be instrumental in obliterating material learned yesterday, last week, or last year.

Proactive inhibition is just the opposite. This is the interference of earlier learning with later learning. In this case, your having learned the names of the first three or four people makes it difficult for you to remember the names of the fifth or sixth. You get them "all mixed up" and maybe cannot recall or even recognize any of them. With either proactive or retroactive inhibition, forgetting is not simply the fading away of memory traces because of disuse. It is, rather, the interaction of new experiences with older ones so that the old is not forgotten or the new is not easily retained.

Proactive inhibition helps explain why we sometimes tend to cling to our old ideas or ways of doing things and resist new ideas or procedures. A person who has learned to drive a car with an automatic transmission, for example, might forget to shift or even forget how to shift for the first few (or several) times he drives a car with a manual transmission. Likewise, having learned rather thoroughly one point of view we might have difficulty in learning another.

Proactive inhibition is at least distantly related to preconception and prejudice. Suppose, for example, that in the elementary grades and high school you learned that Benedict Arnold was an out and out creep, a lousy traitor, a dirty rat. Now suppose that in college you learn about his heroic achievements at Saratoga and the significant positive contributions he made to the patriots' cause early in the War for Independence. Chances are that you would have more than a little difficulty remembering Arnold's positive achievements because of what you had previously learned about his treachery. Of course, retroactive inhibition could also be at work in this case. Learning something about his good points might cause you to forget how "all bad" you previously thought he was.

MOTIVATED FORGETTING

Two other explanations of forgetting, which are closely enough related to be considered together, are suppression and repression.

Both are referred to as "motivated" or "purposeful" because they apply to situations in which we forget because we consciously or unconsciously want to forget. Both are regarded as defense or ego-protective mechanisms in that they are employed to guard the self against some threat or to escape, at least temporarily, some disturbing circumstance.

Suppression is a conscious, deliberate attempt on the part of a person to forget an unpleasant experience. If you have ever said to yourself, with respect to some disappointing or embarrassing experience, "I won't let myself think about it," or "I'll try to forget it," you have made use of suppression. Sometimes it works. More often, perhaps, it only serves to intensify the painful memory.

Repression is an unconscious process. Here the person wants to forget an unpleasant experience but he is not consciously aware of wanting to do so. Repression is basic to the entire system of Freudian psychoanalysis. According to Freud, the id, which is the name he gave to a person's instinctive sex drives or primitive tendencies toward aggressions, gives rise to certain feelings, desires or urges which are socially unacceptable or potentially harmful to the individual himself. The superego, which corresponds roughly to one's conscience, disapproves of these urges and tries to keep them below the threshold of consciousness so that they will not be acted upon. They are said to be repressed.

Feelings of hostility or of sexual attraction toward a parent or a sibling are among the classic Freudian examples of repression. The urge to harm one's father or sister or to make love to one's mother or brother is so repugnant that it never enters the conscious mind at all and the individual is not aware of his ever having had that feeling. If such a repressed urge or some other obnoxious memory or experience does overcome the resistance and enter the person's consciousness, he might try to force it out again by the mechanism of suppression. According to Freud, repressed desires often "disguise" themselves, sometimes elaborately, to secure their release. Thus, if you forget to do something that your mother or some other person asks you to do, a Freudian might suspect that this is your unconscious way of releasing your hostility toward that person.

One need not, of course, accept or even understand Freudian interpretations in order to grasp the concept of motivated forgetting. Many authorities on this subject do not make a distinction between suppression and repression; they speak of them as a single phenomenon which they call repression, but without reference to the unconscious or to any other Freudian concepts. Within or apart from a Freudian framework, repression is of more importance in the areas of mental health and personality development than academic learning. But it does help explain the fact that pleasant experiences, or material learned under pleasant conditions, are likely to be better and longer remembered than those with unpleasant implications or associations. Who knows for sure? Maybe one reason you have forgotten so much of the chemistry you learned in high school is the fact that you intensely disliked your chemistry teacher, or the smell in the chemistry lab.

DISTORTIONS

Forgetting frequently involves some form of distortion. These distortions are of two main kinds: disintegration and assimilation.

Disintegration is the forgetting of some of the details of a learning experience with a clear, and maybe even a clearer, recollection of the "whole picture" or of certain features of that picture. Perhaps at one time you were able to name several signers of the Declaration of Independence, for example, but have since forgotten many or most of those names. But very likely you have a richer, fuller, deeper understanding of that document now than you did then.

Assimilation is the selective retention of certain aspects of a learning experience with elimination of some details and perhaps the addition of others which were not present in the original situation. An adult recalling his prowess as a high school baseball player might really have forgotten the many times he struck out with the bases loaded, but recalls in vivid detail the many game-winning homeruns he hit. Whether he actually did indeed hit all of those home runs, whether he just imagines that he did, or whether he just added a few details to make a better story, I would not want to say. But there is at least the possibility that he assimilated someone else's achievements with his own.

Assimilation and disintegration ordinarily take place together,

149

along with suppression or repression perhaps, to distort our recollections of past experiences. Ordinarily we are likely to retain material or details that are consistent with our existing values, beliefs or attitudes longer and better than material which is threatening, distasteful or at variance with our established, cherished views. Material is best retained, in other words, when it fits our existing frame of reference and proves to be positively reinforcing. One who is favorably disposed toward the Democratic party, for example, might remember more about historical events in which the Democrats made constructive contributions to the country's welfare than he does about events in which they did not do as well. Thus, material which is consciously or unconsciously distorted or selected for retention is not uncommonly related to a person's goals or purposes.

STUDYING FOR RETENTION

How much and how well a person remembers depends upon a number of factors: his goals, his mental abilities, his interests, his level of maturation, his background of experiences, and what he has previously learned. Learning in the sense of acquisition and retention also depend on the nature of the material to be learned and the manner in which it is taught. But most of all, retention depends on what the student himself does. In this section I'd like to focus more directly on classroom learning and consider some methods of studying that are likely to be effective in improving the student's retention.

INTENTION TO REMEMBER

Ordinarily we remember best the kinds of things we want to remember, that we purposefully set out to remember because we see some use in remembering them. Thus, a student's predisposition toward the material to be learned, his desire to remember it, his determination to try to remember it, is all but essential for effective study. This predisposition or intention is commonly referred to as one's "set." Improving a student's set is primarily a matter of motivation, which will be discussed in the next chapter. There we will see that classroom motivation consists largely in helping the student perceive the value of the material to be learned and in relating that material to his existing interests, problems, needs, or goals.

One way to motivate a student to study and to try to remember what he has learned is, of course, to inform him that he will be tested on that material. This is by no means the only way or the best way, but it is one very effective way of developing or increasing a student's intention to remember. Perhaps you can make your material so interesting that your students will want to learn it and remember it forever. Perhaps you will be able to convince your students that your material is so worth studying that, even apart from any possibility of a test, they will make every effort to retain it. But perhaps, like the rest of us ordinary mortal teachers, you will occasionally have to resort to tests as a means of stimulating your students to study. When you do, I strongly recommend that you inform them of what it is that you expect them to remember and why you expect them to remember it.

MEANING

The degree and extent to which we remember particular material depends not only on our intention, but also on the personal meaning that the material has for us.

You would, I am sure, find it easier, quicker, and more useful to remember the above sentence than the same words organized in random order: which, to, material, and degree, particular, depends, etc. You would probably find it even more difficult and less productive to remember the same number of nonsense syllables: nif, zug, pab, dit, etc. The point here is that some of the material that some students are expected to remember is no more meaningful to them than these nonsense syllables are to you. Meaningless material can, of course, be learned by rote, and maybe only by rote. Meaningful material, on the other hand, lends itself to logical memory.

If a student is to remember certain material for any length

of time, he needs a good initial understanding of that material. He needs to organize that material in such a way that internal associations can be made and that the general idea stands out. He needs to perceive the relationships within the material and, if at all possible, the connection between the new material and "old" material that he has already acquired and stored away. The meaning of a subject, as we noted in Chapter 4, depends to a great extent on how we perceive its use or its applicability to ourselves or to something that we want to do or be. Thus, personal meaning as a factor affecting retention goes hand in hand with the previously mentioned concept of the learner's intention to remember.

MNEMONICS

Certain material that is well worth remembering and that we would like to remember might not have much meaning. In such cases, we can make use of so-called mnemonic devices. These are particularly useful for rote memory in that they provide a kind of artificial structure or set of associations that we can use as a kind of crutch. They also provide a kind of logic that otherwise would be lacking.

Some mnemonic devices have been used for so long and have been used so widely that they have become part of our cultural heritage. Instead of memorizing in serial order the number of days in each of the twelve months, most of us, I suspect, rely on the mnemonic: Thirty days hath September. . . . Then there is the sentence "Every good boy does fine" that helps us remember that the lines on a musical scale are designated e, g, b, d, f. There is also the word "homes" to help us recall the names of the five Great Lakes.

In addition to some of these old standbys, many of us have invented our own particular props. For example, back in my undergraduate days I learned about two Greek philosophers, one name Parmenides, the other Heraclitus. One believed that everything in the universe is in constant state of change. The other maintained just the opposite, that nothing really changes. I could not seem to remember which philosopher held which of these positions. One happy day I discovered that Heraclitus had a c in his name, which I associated with "change." Luckily, Parmenides includes an n, which I associated with "no change." Disintegration along with some retroactive inhibition having taken place, I do not remember the details of either of their philosophies. But at least I remember in a general way how each stood on the problem of permanence in the universe.

Incidentally, books and magazine articles of the How to Improve Your Memory type almost always center around the use of mnemonic devices, especially those which an individual is able to make up for himself.

WHOLE-PART-WHOLE METHOD

Suppose that I am going over my notes preparing a lecture I am to give tomorrow morning on a subject I have never lectured on before. Suppose further that you are studying, not just casually reading, this chapter because you are going to have a test on it tomorrow afternoon. Both of us have an "intention to remember." Let's assume that in both of our cases, the material has enough "meaning" so that we need not rely on mnemonic devices. How should we proceed? Well, to begin with, either of us can use the "whole" or the "part" method or a combination of the two.

In using the whole method, we study the entire block of material as a unit. We begin by trying to get an overview or a broad, general understanding of the material to be learned. We try to build a skeleton, as it were, on which we can later hang the particular parts. We try to fashion an outline in our minds, if not on paper, that give meaning to the notes or the chapter and will help us remember logical relationships. Thus, without worrying about the details they contain, I read through all the notes I have on the subject without interruption; you read through the chapter from beginning to end. Both of us, of course, are trying to get the general ideas or the "big picture" as soon as possible. Perhaps we will have to repeat the process a couple of times or more until we are satisfied that we have it. But what we expect is that when we comprehend the general outline, the parts will fall into place, the details will take care of themselves.

When the part method is used, the material is broken down

into sections or subdivisions or particular ideas and we concentrate on each of them one at a time. Thus, you try to get the first page of the chapter "down pat" before going on to the second. Your try to master the section on "Storage and Retrieval" before beginning the section on "Interference." You go over the material on interference as often as you think necessary; then you tackle whatever comes next.

Neither the whole nor the part method has been proved to be better than the other. I might do better with one and you with the other. What I recommend and use myself is a combination of the two, the so-called Whole-Part-Whole method. Here we begin by trying to get an overview of the whole chapter, perhaps just by skimming through it quickly and noting the main headings and subheadings. Then, having completed this survey, we read through the chapter rather carefully paying particular attention to the particular parts that we think deserve or require special concentration. Finally, we conclude by reviewing the chapter as a whole, putting all of the parts together so as to end up with a clearer understanding of the relationships among the concepts and principles it contains than we had after the initial cursory reading.

SPACED AND UNSPACED LEARNING

Now let's suppose that being an efficient, well-organized student you have budgeted your time as your teachers have advised you to do. You find that you have five hours this week that you can devote to studying for an important test. How best to distribute those five hours? Would it be better to study for five consecutive hours on Wednesday night (when none of your favorite TV shows is on) and get it over with? Or would it be more advantageous to spread out your time allotment and spend an hour a night for five nights on the task? What about ten study sessions of a half hour each, or 20 sessions of 15-minute duration? This problem has to do with the relative merits of spaced and unspaced learning.

Spaced (or distributed) learning refers to several short study sessions. Unspaced (or massed) learning refers to fewer but longer sessions. Almost without exception, experimental studies have demonstrated that spaced learning is likely to be more advantageous than unspaced study provided that the study session is not too short. But how short is too short? This, of course, depends, among many other things, upon the nature of the material to be learned.

In general, spaced learning lends itself to the part method and unspaced to the whole. Suppose, for example, that you have a list of 100 discrete items such as foreign language vocabulary to learn. Instead of trying to learn them all at one sitting, you would probably do better to concentrate on, say, ten at a time. Several study sessions of five or ten minutes each would probably be quite productive. Even a couple of minutes now and then, while waiting for a bus or standing in the cafeteria line, could be very helpful in learning such small segments.

With other more complex material, a few minutes at a time might not be nearly enough. Material that is cumulative in nature or rather abstract or that demands sustained attention might better be approached by means of the whole method. The whole method does not, of course, imply using your whole five hours consecutively. But it does suggest study periods of longer duration than ten or fifteen minutes. It might take you a lot longer than that just to get warmed up to the task, to gather your material together, to get yourself settled, and to establish an appropriate mental set.

While I cannot be precise in suggesting the exact number and duration of study sessions that you should use, I can and do recommend the general principle of spaced learning along with the implied practice of frequent review.

CRAMMING VERSUS FREQUENT REVIEW

You have undoubtedly been advised on a number of occasions not to cram for tests, but rather to make use of frequent review. And you have probably ignored this advice, so I am not going to offer it again. Cramming, you will recognize, is essentially a highly concentrated form of unspaced learning. Whatever the objections to cramming might be, there is one thing in its favor: it works. Sometimes.

I have no intention of alienating my colleagues in the teaching profession by recommending that you cram. But you know, perhaps better than I do, that for such short-term purposes as test taking, a concentrated effort at learning a great deal of material in a short space of time just before the occasion on which you will be expected to recall or recognize or paraphrase that material sometimes gets the desired results. Since you have no doubt already been advised that for lasting retention frequent review is likely to be far more effective, I will not repeat that advice.

One of the arguments against cramming is the belief that rapid learning and rapid forgetting go together. "Easy come, easy go." If you learn something quickly, you will forget it quickly. Such really does not seem to be the case. A more valid generalization is that when a person learns something quickly, he is likely to retain it better and longer. The main reason for the positive correlation between rate of acquisition and amount of retention is not the method of studying which is used, but the mental abilities of the individual learner. Regardless of the methods of study they employ, brighter students are likely to learn faster and remember better than their less gifted counterparts.

OVERLEARNING

Closely related to spaced learning and frequent review is the concept of overlearning. Overlearning is usually defined as the continued study of a subject beyond the point of minimal comprehension or beyond the point where recall is barely possible. The concept implies reviewing material or continuing to practice a skill after it has already been learned. Overlearning helps explain why psychomotor skills are usually not forgotten even though they have not been used for a long period of time. As a child, I overlearned to ride a bicycle. I continued to practice or review the skills involved long after I had initially acquired them. The effects have apparently been lasting; after not having ridden one for many years, my first attempt to do so as an adult met with what I regard as considerable success.

Much of our overlearning is unintentional. As very young children, we probably did not intentionally set out to overlearn our names or the names of people or objects in our immediate environment, but through continued repetition we have learned them so well that we'll probably never forget them. Similarly, we have overlearned reading, writing, and other skills, concepts, etc. Even now, as adults, with new material that we regard as very important and hope to retain for a long time, we might choose to continue to "go over" it time and again until it becomes a permanent part of us. As teachers, we might wish to devote some of our efforts toward helping students not only learn, but overlearn.

SELF-RECITATION

Having just made reference to the practice of "going over" material again and again, we should recognize that the continued reading and re-reading of one's notes or textbook is usually not the most efficient way of putting one's study time to good use. More highly recommended is the practice that has been called self-testing or self-recitation. When this method is used, the learner pauses periodically to find out how much of what he has read he remembers. Or in some other way he tests himself or, in effect, recites to himself. As an alternative, he might recite to a parent or friend with whom he has been studying.

Self-recitation takes a variety of forms. In studying Spanish, for example, you might cover the English translations of the words on your vocabulary list and check your ability to recall them. After reading a chapter of your textbook, instead of reading it again, you might formulate in your mind, or better yet on paper, a few questions about the content and see how well you can do in answering them. At this point, for example, you could pause and ask yourself, "Now, let's see. What are mnemonics? What's the difference between spaced and unspaced learning? What do I remember about repression? What was the name of that acid that has something to do with memory?"

One of the best suggestions I can offer my students for preparing for a test is that they formulate a list of questions that they might be asked and then attempt to answer them. Making up the questions, in fact, could be even more productive than supplying the answers. As an alternative, I recommend that they quiz one another. To help them in this regard, I also recommend that in courses or subject areas where it is feasible to do so, the students be given a kind of sample list, or better yet an actual list, of questions from which test items will be drawn. This practice, I believe, not only serves to encourage self-recitation, but also gives the student a better idea of what kinds of things he is expected to remember.

THE TRANSFER OF LEARNING

Teachers ordinarily expect that their students will not only remember but be able to apply material learned in their classes to other classes and to situations outside the school. The English teacher, for example, very likely expects that the knowledge of language usage he has taught his students will help them express their ideas more clearly in, say, a social studies class. The social studies teacher, in turn, very likely hopes that her students will apply the principles of good citizenship that they learned about in her class to their behavior at home and in their community. Teachers might indeed expect and hope for these kinds of carryover, but unfortunately they do not always take place.

The carryover of application of knowledge, skills, attitudes, habits, etc., from the situation in which they were acquired to other situations is called transfer. When the carryover is beneficial to future learning or future behavior, the transfer is said to be positive. When material is applied in such a way that it is detrimental to future behavior or interferes with future learning, the transfer is said to be negative. A simple example of positive transfer would be the case of a child who, having learned to spell the word *light* correctly, applies the appropriate rule and spells *night* correctly without having been specifically taught that word. Negative transfer can be illustrated by the same child who, having learned to spell *night* correctly, thereafter refers to King Arthur's associates at the Round Table as Nights or spells *bite* "bight."

HOW TRANSFER TAKES PLACE

Transfer from one situation to another is most likely to occur when the specifics of the two situations are very much alike. The more they have in common, the greater the amount of transfer that can be expected. Learning to ride a three-speed bicycle, for example, would probably help a person ride a ten-speed bicycle, but let's not forget the possibility of negative transfer or proactive inhibition. The carryover from riding a bicycle to riding a motorcycle might be considerable, but less than that from riding one kind of bike to another. We might expect some transfer from bicycle riding to automobile driving, but not a great deal. Still less, because of the greater dissimilarity, would we expect transfer of bicycle riding to airplane piloting—but even there, a certain amount of transfer might be involved.

Transfer occurs when the "old" and the "new" situations have similar or identical content or require similar or identical procedures. Thus, the study of Latin can help a person with the study of English to the extent that the two languages have similar vocabulary roots or grammatical constructions, or to the extent that the process of learning the one is similar to the process of learning the other. Learning to play a piano should help a person learn to play an organ and perhaps to a lesser degree a guitar. Learning to read should help a person learn to write; learning the geography of the United States should help him learn the history of the country, etc.

In some situations transfer involves a direct application of a principle or a concept from one area to another as, for example, when a student relates his knowledge of the geographical location of Kansas and Nebraska to the events leading up to the Civil War. More commonly, transfer involves the process of generalization. That is to say, much transfer results from the application of general rules, principles, ideas or even attitudes to particular instances. Moral instruction, for example, is not a matter of telling the individual in advance specifically what to do in each and every situation that might arise in his life. It is, rather, a matter of helping him learn to understand and himself apply general moral principles such as those implicit in the Golden Rule. Knowing what the Golden Rule is, however, does not guarantee that the individual will apply it. Just as the student needs help with the acquisition and retention aspects of learning, so does he need help with respect to the applications.

FACILITATING TRANSFER

Education implies the transfer of both products (that is, content or subject matter) and processes of learning (such as methods of thinking and means of acquiring, organizing, and retaining knowledge.) Some students, of course, can and do transfer some products and some processes pretty much on their own, just as they learn by discovery with little or no help from their teachers. But usually transfer does not take place automatically unless the new and old situations are very much alike. Its occurrence, therefore, cannot be taken for granted. Transfer takes place only to a limited extent and only under certain conditions. The amount of transfer that occurs depends on such factors as the nature of the material, the abilities of the learner, and the objectives and methods of the teacher. Let's consider the teacher's objectives as they relate to the facilitation of transfer.

Here, for example, is a science teacher who wants to do more for her students than simply to acquaint them with certain scientific facts, principles or laws. She wants them to do more than simply retain this information. She wants them to learn more than the mechanical routine of laboratory procedures and the use of equipment in carrying out particular kinds of experiments. So she consciously and deliberately formulates her objectives in terms of transfer and teaches accordingly. She wants her students to be able to apply these scientific principles to themselves and to life as they know it outside the school. So she tries to help her students learn the scientific method of problem solving in such a way that they will want to, and be able to, use it outside the laboratory in connection with, say social problems. She might be particularly concerned with developing habits of careful observation and intellectual honesty which her students will generalize and apply in nonscientific situations. One of her important goals might be to develop in her students an understanding of and respect for scientific proof and evidence which they will apply television commercials that use these concepts so loosely and deceptively.

Similarly, the basketball coach might aim at something more than proficiency in the specific skills required for winning basketball games. One of his main objectives might well be to develop in his athletes such old fashioned traits as fair play, good sportsmanship or character. Running around a basketball court, of course, does not automatically bring about good character any more than sitting in a science class teaches a person to think scientifically. Simply aiming at or expecting or hoping for transfer is not enough.

160

SUGGESTIONS FOR TEACHERS

In planning your work as a teacher, here are a few general strategies that you might want to keep in mind and transfer to your particular grade level or subject area.

Try to select as material to be taught and learned ideas, skills, and principles that have widespread potential applicability to the lives of your students either immediately or in the foreseeable future. This, of course, is essentially what is meant by trying to make your material relevant. Point out the relevance of your material or better yet, perhaps through discussions, have them recognize its applicability and explain to one another how it can be used. If it cannot be used or has very limited applicability, ask yourself why you are teaching it and why you expect your students to learn it.

Assuming that the material is worth learning, be sure that your students learn it well in the first place, and that they have a clear understanding of the principles or concepts you would like them to transfer. To be sure that they do, have them verbalize those principles in their own words. When feasible, instead of simply stating the principle, give them the opportunity and the necessary support to discover it on their own. As was suggested in Chapter 4, when a student finds something out by and for himself, the probability is that he will not only retain it longer and better, but that he will be more likely and more able to transfer it.

Provide a variety of examples to illustrate how the material you are teaching can be used and have your students formulate original examples of their own. Point out how your subject is related to other subjects they have studied, or how this unit ties in with other units. Do not assume that they will automatically see the connection between, say, critical thinking or good citizenship in the classroom and opportunities for similar behaviors outside the classroom. Do not even assume that they will recognize that a particular idea or individual that they are learning about in your class is the very same idea or person they might have encountered in some other class.

Relate the new idea or principle at first to situations which are as much like the original as possible, and then gradually to other situations which are progressively less similar. But insofar as possible, let your students try to find the relationships and do the applying. In this regard, your main function should be to give them the opportunities to practice using what they have learned and to transfer it to as many different kinds of situations as possible. In short, remember that if your students have not learned to use the knowledge, skills, attitudes or whatever it is that you have been teaching, they really have not learned it at all.

SUMMARY

Although learning certainly involves much more than memorizing, retention is an indispensable aspect of the total learning process. While rote memorization of certain material can serve a useful purpose, logical memory is ordinarily preferred. Logical memory presumes an understanding of meaningful associations. Retention implies not only the storage of experiences, but also some system of retrieving them when they are needed.

Exactly how much foregetting takes place and how rapidly we forget depends not only on such factors as the nature and meaning of the material, and on the individual's memory abilities, but also on the system of retrieval and the method of measuring retention that is employed. The relearning method usually shows considerably more retention than do recall or recognition methods. Among the major reasons for forgetting, in addition to disuse, are interference (retroactive and proactive inhibition), the desire to forget (suppression or repression), and memory distortion (disintegration and assimilation).

Retention of classroom material depends to a great extent on one's methods of studying. Generally recommended in this respect are a firm intention to remember, a clear understanding of the material, the use of the whole-part-whole method, spaced learning, frequent review, overlearning, self-recitation, and the occasional use of mnemonics. Much of the guesswork can be taken out of studying and the process made more efficient if students are informed of what it is that they will be expected to recall or recognize at some future date for testing purposes.

Effective learning presumes not only the retention, but also the application, or transfer, or use of material that has been acquired. Transfer takes place from one situation to another when the new and old situations have something in common. In such cases, the student is able to generalize or carry over his knowledge, skills, or attitudes from the one to the other. Transfer is not an automatic process, which is why teachers should consciously aim at, and teach for, applicability.

Recommended Readings

Bower, Gordon H. "How to. . .Uh. . .Remember!" *Psychology Today.* October, 1973. An interesting and informative article that includes a number of suggestions for the improvement of retention through the use of mnemonics.

Ellis, Henry C. "Transfer and Retention." In Melvin H. Marx, ed. *Learning Processes.* New York: Macmillan, 1969. Summarizes a wealth of information about the nature and measurement of transfer and retention, explains these two fundamental processes, and interprets pertinent research findings.

Ericksen, Standford. *Motivation for Learning.* Ann Arbor: University of Michigan Press, 1974. Despite the title, this book is mentioned here because of its chapters on transfer, grading, and evaluation. Intended for teachers at the college level, it also has a chapter on "how to think."

Krech, David. "Psychoneurobiochemeducation." *Phi Delta Kappan,* March, 1969. This is a very readable article on brain chemistry as it relates to memory and learning. Reviews some of the research and speculates about what the future holds in this regard.

Kumar, V.K. "The Structure of Human Memory and Some Educational Implications." *Review of Educational Research,* December, 1971. Summarizes research findings about the nature of retention and forgetting, and discusses their implications for education.

Ladas, Harold. "Grades: Standardizing the Unstandardized Standards." *Phi*

Delta Kappan. November, 1974. The author argues that grades should be based solely on measurable scholastic achievement, not on effort, attendance, attitudes, self-concept improvement, etc. This article is followed by a response, written by Neil Postman, entitled "A D+ for Mr. Ladas."

Policastro, Michael. "Notetaking: The Key to College Success." *Journal of Reading.* Feb., 1975. A short article that compares three methods of note-taking. Might help you study more effectively.

Sahakian, William S. *Psychology of Learning.* Chicago: Markham, 1970. Part III contains an abundance of primary source material on various theories of memory and research in the area. Hardly light reading, but recommended for the reader who is seriously interested in the subject of retention and forgetting.

8

Motivation for Learning

Of all the factors that have a bearing on the quality and quantity of a person's learning, two of the most critical are his abilities and his desire to learn. If you have enough determination to learn a particular subject and the necessary abilities to do so, you almost certainly will learn it, even with an incompetent teacher or perhaps with no teacher at all. Most students have the necessary abilities to learn but they do not always use them. We shall take up the subject of learning abilities and disabilities in the next chapter. In this one, we shall consider the desire-determination-motivation aspects of learning.

HUMAN NEEDS AND GOALS

Why is it that some students study and others do not? Why is it that some want to learn and try to learn while others apparently have little or no interest in doing so? Why, for that matter, does anyone do anything?

In trying to answer questions such as these, there are two basic principles to keep in mind. One is the principle, discussed in Chapter 3, that "behavior is shaped by its consequences." According to this principle, the principle of reinforcement, we do things that are likely to have pleasant consequences and avoid behaviors that are likely to be followed by unpleasant consequences. The second principle is that human behavior is directed toward the satisfaction of certain needs or the attainment of certain goals. These two principles are complementary rather than contradictory or mutually exclusive, since the satisfaction of a need is ordinarily a pleasant consequence while the failure to attain a goal is generally perceived as unpleasant. But let's use the second of these principles as a point of departure for the discussion of human motivation that follows.

KINDS OF NEEDS

Human needs and the corresponding goals have been categorized in various ways and a variety of labels have been employed to designate them. For our present purposes, we can classify them, as Abraham Maslow and a number of other psychologists have done, under five main headings: physiological, safety, love, esteem, and self-actualization.

Physiological needs include such things as food, clothing, and shelter which are necessary for our very survival. These, of course, are the most basic of all, pertaining as they do to self-preservation in the strict biological sense of the term.

Safety needs refer to our feeling of assurance that these basic survival needs will be satisfied in the future. These needs are largely economic in nature, but they border on, or overlap with, our needs for emotional security.

Love, as we are using the term here, is essentially a feeling of emotional security. It implies a need for affection and affiliation. It includes the feeling that somebody cares about us and values us for our own sake.

Esteem refers to a person's need to feel important, worthwhile, looked up to, respected, admired. It implies the need for attention, recognition, status, prestige, or something of that sort.

Self-actualization refers to an individual's striving for personal growth or fulfillment, his need to become to the fullest extent possible himself, to develop his potentialities, to become what he is capable of becoming. Self-actualization implies one's need for self-expression, aesthetic experience, enjoyment, and one's need to know, to satisfy his curiosity, to understand himself, other people, and the world around him.

Most human behavior, in the classroom or elsewhere, has as its purpose the satisfaction of one or another or some combination of these five kinds of needs. Anything that contributes to the satisfaction of these needs is said to be reinforcing. Strictly speaking, there is no such thing as an unmotivated student or a person in any walk of life who lacks motivation. All human beings are always motivated in that we all have needs, we all have goals. We all have essentially the same kinds of needs and the same kinds of goals. But we differ in the ways we choose to satisfy them and in our perceptions of what constitutes satisfaction.

Thus, every student is motivated—but not necessarily to learn to do what his teachers would like him to do. The goals he wishes to pursue here and now are not necessarily the ones she wants him to pursue in the classroom. The manner in which he attempts to satisfy his needs is not necessarily the manner that she would prefer. This is why we have motivation "problems." To help students who are not highly motivated toward scholastic achievement, it might be well to consider the goals of those who are.

APPROVAL

Perhaps the most common goal of students who do well in school is approval, which roughly corresponds to the need for love. This goal is likely to be particularly characteristic of younger children who want and need the approval or affection of their parents and their teachers, and who are so very dependent upon these adults for the satisfaction of that need. Children frequently perceive scholastic achievement as one of the few ways or even as the best way they can earn approval.

Consider, for example, a child who does not especially like mathematics. In fact, he detests it. He has no interest in the subject and sees no value in it. But he applies himself industriously to the learning of mathematics simply because it is expected of him, because his parents and teacher want him to, because it is a means of gaining or maintaining their approval. Note that approval, not the learning of mathematics, is his primary goal. Note also that the attainment of that goal or the satisfaction of the corresponding need constitutes what we have previously referred to as reinforcement.

Some high school and college students are also motivated at least in part by their need or desire for approval. They do not want to disappoint or displease their parents or "let them down." But the approval motive is likely to be stronger in younger than in older students. The adolescent is ordinarily more concerned with gaining the approval of his peer group than that of his parents or teachers, and adolescent peer groups are not likely to award him many points for scholastic achievement. In fact, they might actually deduct points for such things as high grades or other symptoms of "braininess."

Everyone has a need for approval, but some younger as well as older children do not get much of it for good schoolwork, even from their parents. Consider, for example, the child who receives little or no praise, encouragement or positive reinforcement for scholastic achievement from his parents, teachers, friends, or anyone else. His parents only glance perfunctorily at his report card. They pay no attention to the completed work he brings home. They show no interest in his progress. They indicate, perhaps only by their silence, that they do not think school work is particularly important. I doubt very much that such a child will continue for very long to try to satisfy this need by striving for scholastic success. More likely, he will try to find some other way of winning parental approval, or focus his efforts on winning the approval of his peers.

RECOGNITION

A second important goal of students who are highly motivated toward scholastic achievement is recognition, which corresponds

170

to the need for esteem. Here I have in mind a student who sees no value in a particular subject, who does not enjoy it, who has no great interest in it. He is not working for approval because he has already satisfied this need. He has learned that his parents love him and will continue to love him regardless of what he does or fails to do in school. But he works hard and is very much concerned with getting good grades. His purpose in doing so might be to impress someone, to gain their favorable attention, to be well thought of. Very likely he wants to prove to others (his teachers, for example, or perhaps his parents or friends) that he cannot only succeed in his school work, but that he can actually surpass the others in his class. Maybe his craving for recognition is so strong that he is unwilling to settle for anything less than being Number One.

This type of student needs good grades—or some other form of recognition—in order to bolster his ego, strengthen his self-concept, develop his feeling of personal worth or something of that sort. He wants to feel that he is at least as good as his classmates, and maybe even better. He not only wants to be recognized and admired, but maybe even envied. As is the case with approval, anything that contributes to the individual's need for recognition tends to serve as a powerful reinforcer.

As is the case with approval, everyone has a need for recognition, but for some young people scholastic achievement is not a particularly promising means of getting it. One who finds the work too difficult, for example, is likely to become discouraged, recognize that he cannot compete successfully, give up trying, withdraw from the situation psychologically, and to protect his ego display an "I don't care" kind of attitude. If he lacks or feels that he lacks the necessary ability to do well in school, or if he does not have enough self-confidence to even try, he will certainly be looking for some other means of gaining recognition—as the class clown, for example, or in sports or social activities, or, for that matter, in antisocial activities. If one can gain recognition with approval, fine. But recognition with disapproval might be perceived as more desirable than no recognition at all.

Recognition, like approval, is undoubtedly a major purpose of some students who are said to be highly motivated in their classrooms. Both of these needs can be used as effective incentives with those who are not highly motivated initially. They underlie most of the practical classroom strategies that will be discussed

171

later in this chapter. But these same two goals also help explain why certain students are, or appear to be, "unmotivated" with respect to classroom learning.

PRACTICAL VALUES

Instead of, or in addition to, striving to satisfy their needs for approval or recognition or both, many students are motivated toward scholastic achievement by what they regard as the practical value of the subject or skill they are expected to learn. I do not suppose that there are many students whose main purpose in learning to drive a car, for example, is to gain approval or recognition. These might be among their secondary purposes, but I suspect that most recognize the immediate practical use of automobile driving. If the uses of English literature, biology, history, etc., were that apparent, teachers of those subjects would, as their students might put it, "have it made."

Adolescents do not ordinarily ask "what good" automobile driving will "do" them. Nor are elementary school students likely to inqure why they have to learn to read and write. The practical values of these accomplishments need not be spelled out. They are readily perceived as means to social and financial success. Without stretching the point too much we can think of such basic skills as "bread and butter" matters, and relate them to the individual's physiological and safety needs.

At the high school and college levels, when careers are becoming a matter of some concern, the practical value of subjects are likely to be called into question. It is then that students are more likely to ask "what good" certain subjects are. If they see the use of a subject in relationship to their vocational goals, chances are they will work at it.

Here is a high school student who has his heart set on becoming an engineer. Even though he does not especially enjoy physics, he is quite willing to study it because he sees the need for that subject as a means to his vocational goal. But what about American history? He does not see how that subject will help him as an engineer. But he studies it diligently because it is required for the diploma he is seeking or because he has been told (perhaps incorrectly) that he "needs it" in order to be admitted to a particular college of engineering. Thus, while the practical value of history is, for him, not as direct as that of physics, he still perceives it as having this indirect, practical value.

Just as it would be a mistake to rely excessively or exclusively on the student's need for approval or recognition as a motivational strategy, so would it be unreasonable to try to justify every subject in terms of its practical value, particularly if we limit our usage of the word practical to that which is immediately useful or financially rewarding. But in a broader sense, every subject has at least some potential value as a means of helping the individual live a richer, fuller, happier life regardless of his occupation. Ordinarily when students perceive this value, they are motivated to learn the subject; when they do not, they are not.

INTRINSIC MOTIVATION

A distinction is commonly made between intrinsic and extrinsic motivation. These forms of motivation correspond approximately to interest and incentives, which we shall discuss later in this chapter. With respect to intrinsic motivation, we might recognize at this point those students who want to learn, not primarily to satisfy their needs for approval or recognition and not primarily for the purpose of gaining economic security or vocational success, but simply because they want to. These individuals perceive knowledge not so much as a tool or a stepping stone or a means to an end, but as an end in itself. For them, learning is its own reward, an activity that is satisfying in and of itself, much as they might find singing in the shower or smelling a flower or sipping good wine as intrinsically worthwhile, needing no other justification, and having no other "purpose."

Intrinsically motivated students might incidentally gain recognition or approval for their efforts and they might incidentally put the knowledge they acquire to some practical use. But such "fringe benefits" are, for them, only incidental. The type of student I have in mind reads history books, for example, or works mathematical problems because he finds these activities interesting, enjoyable and personally fulfilling. He does not need

173

any incentives to pursue these activities. He neither wants nor expects any external reinforcement for doing so. His reinforcement comes first and foremost from within himself, which is why he is said to be inner rather than outer directed. His main goal, in short, is self-actualization.

CLASSROOM MOTIVATIONAL STRATEGIES

Most teachers, I am sure, would love to have a room full of intrinsically motivated students, eager to learn simply for the love of learning. But many teachers, particularly in the upper elementary grades and beyond, encounter few such individuals in their classes. Many teachers, therefore, find that one of their most challenging problems is that of arousing their students' interests, gaining and holding their attention, and somehow prevailing upon them to set forth at least a little effort in learning the material they are expected to learn even when they are not exactly overjoyed at the prospect of learning it. The two basic strategies that teachers employ in attacking the motivation problem center around the concepts of interest and incentives.

INTEREST

Interest, as has been suggested, corresponds to intrinsic motivation. You are said to be interested in an activity when your motives for engaging in that activity, or attending to that activity, come from within yourself. If you are truly interested in folk music, for example, no one has to "motivate" you to listen to it. If you are interested in literature, you enjoy reading and no bribes or threats, external pressures or inducements are necessary to cause you to read.

A good example of an inherently interesting activity is practically any form of what we call "play." Now, a professional athlete might "play" football primarily because of the financial remuneration he receives as a consequence. In that case, his motivation is extrinsic, money is his incentive, and his activity might more appropriately be referred to as work. Most of us, however, are not paid to play football or bridge or Scrabble or whatever it is that we do play. Most children, and for that matter most adults, play because they want to, because they are interested in the activity itself, because they find the activity a source of relaxation or pleasure or enjoyment or even of personal fulfillment.

But interest does not always or necessarily imply pleasure or enjoyment, recreation or fun. I do not suppose that you would derive any pleasure from hearing about a series of burglaries in your neighborhood or the illness of a close friend, but you would certainly be interested in these matters. Why? Because somehow they affect you personally. Somehow they have or might have or could have some bearing on your life, your welfare, your happiness, or your something else. If these things do not directly affect you personally, they do directly affect your friends or neighbors who are, in a sense, an extension of yourself.

Thus, interest, as I am presently using that word, is essentially a matter of perceiving a relationship between oneself and some event or situation or possibility outside oneself. When we recognize this relationship, we are interested whether the situation is pleasurable or not. Ordinarily the stronger or closer the relationship, the greater our interest.

Most of us, I suspect, would not be nearly as interested in a burglary that occurred a thousand miles away as we would be in one next door—unless the victim of the distant burglary were someone in whom we already had a strong interest. Most of us are not as interested in the outcome of a basketball game being played by strangers from out of town as we are when our friends, classmates or we ourselves are members of the team, or when the team somehow represents our school or our city. Even if our team loses, we are interested in knowing the outcome of the game. Similarly, we are interested in, or care about, the outcome of a movie or a novel to the extent that we somehow identify with one or some of the characters. Indirectly, vicariously, what affects them, affects us.

Whatever it might be that you are presently interested in, your interests were not innate. They were acquired. You were not born with an interest in sports or science or fictional characters, or even in the welfare of your friends. You learned to be interested in these things. Your existing interests, in turn, have had an effect on your subsequent learning and on your acquisition of new interests. Thus, interests can be thought of as both causes and effects of learning. Just as they are the products of previous learning so are they also a means of facilitating future learning.

DEVELOPING INTERESTS

Although it is by no means essential for a person to be interested in a subject in order to learn it, it is generally assumed that interest helps. One of the things that teachers are expected to do, therefore, is "make" schoolwork interesting.

Making school work interesting, as has been suggested, is not necessarily or primarily a matter of making it all fun and games. Not that there is anything wrong with fun and games in a classroom, but contrary to what some students seem to expect, the teacher's job is not to amuse them. Schools are not established and maintained as recreation centers. Teachers are not employed to act as professional entertainers. If a teacher can use fun and games to help his students learn, he certainly should not hesitate to use them. If he can keep his students entertained without diluting the quality of their work or his, well and good. But overemphasis on the fun aspect of learning has caused more than a few teachers to confuse means with ends, and to miss the main point of what it means to develop and maintain interests. The fun and games approach to classroom motivation, in fact, can become positively boring and intellectually stultifying.

Developing interest in a subject, as I see it, is primarily a matter of helping the student see how the material he is expected to learn relates to him as an individual. This process involves showing the student, or helping the student herself discover, how this knowledge or these skills affect her, how the material can serve her purposes, how it can help satisfy her physical or safety needs, her needs for recognition and approval, or how it can help her directly or indirectly to fulfill herself as a complete person. When the student realizes that learning is a means toward the achievement of some goal that she considers important, when she foresees that the result of the learning experience will somehow make a positive difference to her personally, she will be interested in, and motivated toward, learning it.

One of the most effective ways of stimulating interest in a new subject is to build on the student's existing interests. It is important, therefore, that teachers know what the present interests of their students are. If a student is interested in current political or social problems, for example, his history teacher should certainly try to capitalize on that interest. If a student is interested in baseball batting averages, his math teacher might do well to use that interest as a means of developing an interest in the computation of percentages. New interests are rarely, if ever, created out of the blue. They are, rather outgrowths of previously acquired interests.

An individual's particular interests will depend, of course, upon a number of variables such as his age, sex, mental abilities, socioeconomic status, the interests of his family and friends, the kind of community in which he lives, and the opportunities he has had for acquiring new interests and cultivating old ones. But every person, regardless of any of these variables, has an interest in himself, his human needs and his general goals. Self-interest, therefore, would seem to be the one constant factor that can serve as a foundation upon which many new interests can be built.

THE TEACHER AS A SALESPERSON

With respect to motivation in general, and making school-work interesting in particular, the teacher's function is not to change the student's goals. She could not do so if she tried. Her function, rather, is to help the student recognize that her purposes and his goals are essentially the same, that she is trying to help him attain the very goals that he himself is seeking, that the material she is teaching is a means of achieving one or some of those goals, and that it is to his advantage to learn it. Hers is essentially a selling job, as she tries to convince her students of the value of her subject and tries to persuade them that it is worth studying.

Ordinarily, a good salesperson believes in her product. A teacher who does not believe in hers is likely to have a difficult time selling it. If she herself is not convinced of the importance of the material she is teaching for her particular students, if she herself cannot see how it will help them or "what good" it will do them, it is not likely that she will be very successful in "making" that work interesting. If, on the other hand, she is highly enthusiastic about the value of her product, there is a good chance that some of her enthusiasm will be contagious.

INCENTIVES

If, as a teacher, you can render your material interesting in the sense of enjoyable or useful or both, you are certainly encouraged to do so. But certain outcomes of learning are considered to be so important that students are expected to learn them whether they are interested in them or not, whether they see any particular value at the moment in learning them or not. If your efforts toward arousing and maintaining interest do not bear fruit, you will probably want to—indeed, you might have to—use some sort of incentive.

Incentives correspond to outer direction and extrinsic motivation. Incentives, of course, are means—such as money—which are employed to induce a person to do something that he otherwise would not do, or would not do as well. Among the more common classroom incentives, as you know, are such devices, as grades and report card marks, prizes, honors, special privileges, etc., which emanate from some source outside the individual himself. These you will recognize as what we referred to in Chapter 3 as positive reinforcers. Negative reinforcers, such as the threat of failure or attempts to avoid unpleasant consequences, also serve as incentives.

Positive incentives used in the classroom are, in effect, immediate rewards which are used as substitutes for, or stepping stones toward, more remote goals. The value of learning certain subjects often lies far in the learner's future, and even then it might be intangible and rather far-fetched. Let's face it. Telling a junior high school student that someday he will be glad he studied this poetry because it will make him a well-rounded person is not likely to prove very effective. But offering him a more tangible reward here and now might do the trick. Note that if it does, the student's goal is not primarily to learn the poetry; it is to attain the immediate rewards. Thus learning becomes a means, and maybe even an obstacle, toward reaching the goal that he is really striving for. Consequently, the student might "work for grades," cram for tests, and maybe even resort to cheating in order to receive his reward, instead of learning for the love of learning, which his teacher might prefer. But that is the chance you have to take. Frankly, I can think of only one good reason for the use of incentives: they work.

In some cases the use of incentives undoubtedly does cause students to study only in order to pass tests and get good grades. But at least they do study and in the process learn something of value. Undoubtedly it would be much nicer if students studied and learned without these extrinsic rewards being dangled in front of them. But realistically, many of them do not and will not. Undoubtedly teachers should make every reasonable effort to develop on the part of their students an interest in the material to be learned. But in addition they can also foster an interest in the incentives they are able to provide. Thus, they can motivate their students toward scholastic achievement indirectly when they are unable to do so directly.

CARROTS AND STICKS

Reward and punishment, praise and scoldings, enticements and threats, positive and negative reinforcement, approval and disapproval, carrots and sticks—these are the oldest motivational devices known to mankind. As we noted in Chapter 3, praise, reward, and approval are likely to be more effective than their opposites as means of motivating students toward scholastic achievement. A number of experimental studies have demonstrated rather conclusively that, in general, students who are regularly and systematically rewarded for their good work or for improvement in the quality of their work tend to do better than those who are scolded or criticized for their poor work or their lack of progress. Threatening a child with failure or punishment for poor school work has not been found to be particularly effective. Frequent punishment and anxiety-producing threats, in fact, have been found to inhibit, rather than promote, learning. Nevertheless, some studies have shown that those who received mild words or signs of disapproval for substandard work generally did better than those who were neither praised nor scolded, but simply ignored.

Other studies have indicated that the source of the approval or disapproval, the frequency of the approval or disapproval, and the personality of the individual student receiving the approval or disapproval makes quite a difference. A compliment or a word of encouragement from one of your friends very likely does not mean the same thing to you that the same word from another does. Similarly, praise or criticism from one teacher probably does not have the same effect on you, or anyone else, as praise or criticism from some other teacher.

Both approval and disapproval can be overdone. Praise from a gushing-type teacher who seems to be constantly praising everyone and everything does not have the same value that it does when it comes from one who is more discriminating and not quite so free and easy with it. Perhaps you have known teachers who are so parsimonious with praise that on the rare occasions when they do compliment a student their compliments are long remembered. On the other hand, reproof from a teacher who is constantly carping and fault-finding ordinarily carries far less weight than criticism from one who is less inclined toward nagging. Of the two, however, there is less danger of overdoing the praise than there is of excessive blame.

The personality of the recipient is also a major factor in determining the relative effectiveness of reward and punishment. Ordinarily, a shy, withdrawing, introverted, insecure type of student responds more positively toward praise than does the self-confident, outgoing, aggressive type of student. Disapproval, on the other hand, is likely to be more effective with the extrovert than the introvert. So the blanket generalization that approval or reward or a carrot is better than disapproval or punishment or a stick does not always hold. Both can and should be used. But when in doubt, you are likely to achieve better results with the carrot.

TANGIBLE REINFORCERS

As we noted in Chapter 3, an object or an experience that is positively reinforcing with one student does not always have a positively reinforcing effect on another. What one person perceives as a reward that is well worth working for might not appeal to another student at all. Not everyone is that fond of carrots. While verbal praise, good grades, etc., have proved to be highly effective with some students, others apparently could not care less about such things. These others might respond more favorably to tangible kinds of incentives such as money or so-called token reinforcers.

Tokens are usually little plastic chips, slips of paper, coupons, trading stamps, "points" on a chart, or something of that sort which are given to students for specified behavior or achievement. Unlike some other kinds of incentives, the tokens are not awarded on a competitive basis. One need not be the first or the best in his class to be rewarded. Each and every child who meets certain conditions—such as scoring at least 80% on a spelling test or improving by at least 10% in arithmetic or doing his homework faithfully or making what the teacher judges to be satisfactory effort—can expect to be rewarded.

A specified number of tokens can be exchanged for candy, toys, comic books, a trip to a museum, free time, or whatever else the teacher can and wants to offer. One of the problems with the use of this "token economy" is finding objects or activities for which the tokens can be exchanged that students will find attractive and that the school or teacher can afford.

BRIBERY

The principle underlying the use of tangible reinforcers is, of course, the same as that of giving children money for good grades or for other desired behaviors. Critics of these practices (and of the use of incentives in general) have referred to them as forms of bribery, but the use of that word in this context does not seem to be justified. Bribery ordinarily implies paying someone secretly for doing something illegal. But there is nothing illegal about learning how to spell, and the token (or money or gold stars) are not given out under the table.

Still there are those who object, sometimes strenuously, for paying students to do what they should do freely. A teacher's

181

life would indeed be beautiful if all of her students were, or could readily be made, intrinsically motivated; or if they did what was expected of them simply because it was expected of them. But that is usually not the way it is in classrooms any more than it is in the professions or the world of business and industry. Most teachers teach for more than the love of teaching (although many of them do love teaching); they teach because of the "tangible reinforcers" they receive in their paychecks.

Similarly, the parents of most students work at whatever jobs they have, not because they are "intrinsically interested" in those jobs, but because of the financial payoff at the end of the week. Perhaps it is not entirely reasonable, therefore, to expect students to differ from their parents and teachers in this respect. I am not especially recommending the use of token reinforcers, or giving students money for scholastic achievement. But neither am I dead set against such practices as a matter of principle. If you can get the desired results from your students without them, I see no reason why you should use them. But if your other efforts at motivation fail, you might want to give them a try.

COMPETITION

Competition has been widely used for centuries as a means of motivation toward scholastic achivement. Generations of students have exerted themselves—as many, of course, still do—to win some sort of prize, to receive the highest grade on a test, to make the dean's list or the honor roll, to have their work selected for posting on the bulletin board, or in some other way to surpass their classmates.

Such effort has been explained as an attempt on the part of the individual to satisfy his need for recognition or esteem. It has also been explained as the sublimination of his aggressive tendencies, as compensation for a feeling of inferiority, as the manifestation of his innate drive toward mastery or domination or achievement, and in numerous other ways. Whatever the theoretical basis of competition might be, it seems clear that human beings enjoy competing with one another, in sports and games, for example, and that competition is unquestionably a significant spur toward commendable accomplishment in business and industry, in the arts and professions, and in many other areas of human endeavor, including education. Since competition so permeates our culture, it has been argued that one of the responsibilities of the school is to teach children how to compete as a means of preparing them for reality. Thus, competition is often regarded not only as an effective means of motivating students scholastically, but also as an activity which is worthwhile in and of itself.

Since the early part of the twentieth century, right down to the present, doubts have been raised about the effectiveness of, and need for, competition. The problem has been put to a number of experimental tests. By and large, competition has been vindicated. Several studies have shown, for example, that students who were encouraged to compete with one another on an individual basis did better scholastically than those who worked as part of a team, cooperating with their teammates, but competing with other teams. In other words, students were found to work harder and make more improvement when they tried to win an individual reward for themselves than they did to win one that would be shared with other members of their group. But even group competition produced better scholastic gains than no competition at all.

OBJECTIONS TO COMPETITION

Despite its demonstrated utility in contributing to scholastic achievement, objections have been raised about the possiblity of adverse side effects of competition on the individual's overall personality and social development. It has been argued, for example, that competition is especially harmful to slow learners. In every form of competition, somebody wins at the expense of somebody else's losing. Unfortunately, it is often the same students who end up as the losers, and this does not do much good for their self-concepts. Thus, it is alleged, competition causes the poorer student to stop trying and to feel even less adequate than he did originally. It is supposed to contribute to feelings of superiority or selfishness or vanity on the part of some students; frustration, discouragement, and a feeling of worthlessness in others. Moreover, it is supposed to cause bitterness, jealousy, resentment, and even hostility among the competitors.

Actually, there is very little, if any, evidence that such fears or suppositions are well-founded. Like anything else, competition can, of course, be overdone and abused. Certainly no child should be forced into a competitive situation when it is a foregone conclusion that he has no chance of winning. It is no more than fair that the contestants be evenly matched. It is just as unrealistic and unfair to expect every member of a class to attain the same level of scholastic achievement as it would be to expect that they should all run at about the same speed or be able to lift the same weight. Perhaps some teachers have gone overboard with regard to competition as others have done with respect to the concept of making learning fun. But the possible excesses of a few teachers should not be allowed to cast serious doubt on the value of either of these strategies.

SELF-COMPETITION

While excessive pressures to achieve under highly competitive circumstances could be injurious to the individual's self-concept as well as his scholastic progress and social relationships, a learning situation with no element of competition at all might be as boring as it would be ineffective. To try to eliminate competition from the classroom entirely would be as unrealistic and undesirable as going to the opposite extreme of overemphasizing competitiveness. A reasonable middle position between these extremes is a form of competition to which no one has raised any serious objections: competition with oneself.

Self-competition is the procedure by which an individual tries to surpass his own past performance without reference to what anyone else does. The key concepts here are progress or improvement, rather than reaching or surpassing the level of performance attained by one's classmates. The student is not subjected to unfavorable comparisons with others. Every student has a chance to achieve some degree of success. Her abilities are taken into account, her self-concept need not be threatened, and she is permitted to advance at her own rate. She is systematically provided with feedback, she might be encouraged to use some sort of chart on which she can plot her progress, and her slightest improvement can be reinforced. This form of competition—if it can or should be called that—is particularly well-suited to attempts at individualizing instruction, a subject that is dealt with at rather great length in our final chapter.

SELF-CONFIDENCE

Self-competition and feedback as means of helping the individual want to try to do better the next time presumes that he will gradually gain confidence in himself and raise what has been called his level of aspiration. One's level of aspiration pertains to the goals he sets for himself, the amount and quality of work he believes he can do and is willing to try to do. Part of a teacher's job in this respect is to help each student set goals for himself which are high enough to be challenging and require a reasonable degree of effort, but are realistic enough to be attainable. If one's level of aspiration is too high, especially in the early stages of learning, he may be letting himself in for unnecessary frustrations. If it is too low, he is likely to slough off, fail to do the kind of work he is capable of, and never have a real opportunity to build up his self-esteem.

A student's self-confidence depends upon a number of factors, chief among them being what he perceives as his teacher's expectations of him, and his own previous record of success and failures. Ordinarily, when teachers demonstrate that they expect a high level of performance on the part of their students, and indicate that they believe their students are quite capable of rising to those standards, the students are likely to gain confidence and work accordingly. When teachers' expectations are low, their students' levels of aspirations might be even lower. Generally speaking, students who have recently experienced success are likely to set goals for themselves which are realistic and higher than their previous levels. Those who have recently experienced failure have been found to set goals which are either unrealistically high or unacceptably low.

For the purposes under discussion, a good policy for a teacher is to begin with work that is relatively easy (but not insultingly so) so that the student can get off to a good start by experiencing a feeling of success and gaining confidence. Then she should gradually increase the degree of difficulty of the work, keeping the student informed of his improvement, and encouraging him to do just a little bit better next time. She should communicate her confidence in his ability to keep improving, and convey her expectation that he will do so. And, of course, she should continue trying to make the work as interesting, enjoyable, and relevant to the student's needs as possible.

Motivating students toward scholastic achievement is not easy. But nowhere in this book have I implied that any aspect of a teacher's job is.

SUMMARY

Most human behavior, in the classroom as elsewhere, has as its purpose the satisfaction of some need or the attainment of a corresponding goal. Anything that contributes to the satisfaction of a need can be considered a reinforcer. All human beings have the same set of needs (physiological, security, love, esteem, and self-actualization), but we differ in the ways we choose to satisfy them, and in our perceptions of what constitutes satisfaction. Many students are reasonably well-motivated toward scholastic achievement by their desire for approval (love), or recognition (esteem), by what they regard as the practical (security) value of the subject, or by the personal satisfaction they derive from the subject itself (self-actualization.)

Classroom motivational strategies center around the concepts of interest and incentives, which correspond to intrinsic and extrinsic motivation respectively. Making schoolwork interesting is not necessarily a matter of making it all fun and games. Rather, it primarily involves helping the student see how the material he is expected to learn relates to him and his goals. In this respect, teachers can either build on students' existing interests or try to "sell" them new ones.

Incentives involve some system of rewards and possibly punishment. Experimental studies have demonstrated rather conclusively that, in general, students who are systematically rewarded for their good work or for improvement tend to do better than those who are scolded for poor work or lack of progress. However, the personalities of the individuals giving and receiving the approval or disapproval might be critical in determining which is more effective in a particular situation.

The practice of offering tangible rewards for scholastic achievement, and the use of incentives in general, has been criticized, as has the use of competition as a motivational device. Despite some legitimate concerns with these practices, they have been found to be quite useful with few, if any, documented, detrimental side-effects, when used reasonably. One of the main purposes of motivational strategies should be to help develop the student's self-confidence and raise his level of aspiration.

Recommended Readings

Day, H.I., and Berlyne, D.E. "Intrinsic Motivation." In G.S. Lesser, ed. *Psychology and Educational Practice*. Glenview, Ill.: Scott, Foresman, 1971. Explains the theory and nature of intrinsic motivation and reviews some of the research on the subject. A large part of the article is devoted to curiosity.

Drew, Walter F. et al. "Motivation Is a Matter of Trust and Dialogue." *Learning*, Jan., 1975. An informal account of how a sixth-grade teacher relies on conversation, mutual trust, and genuine caring as a principal means of maintaining a high level of academic motivation.

Greene, David, and Lepper, Mark. "Intrinsic Motivation: How to Turn Play Into Work." *Psychology Today*, Sept., 1974. Proponents of intrinsic motivation, the authors are highly critical of token reinforcement because, as they claim, it turns what should be play into work.

Johnson, David W., and Johnson, Roger T. *Learning Together and Alone*. Englewood Cliffs, N.J.: Prentice-Hall, 1975. Compares competitive, cooperative, and individualized learning environments and demonstrates how each can be used most effectively in achieving cognitive and affective objectives.

Kolesnik, Walter B. Motivation: Understanding and Influencing Human Behavior. Boston, Mass.: Allyn and Bacon, 1978. Summarizes Freudian, Adlerian, behavioral, cognitive and humanistic theories of motivation, and relates them to classroom management and scholastic achievement.

Maslow, Abraham H. *Motivation and Personality*. 2d ed. New York: Harper and Row, 1970. A unified theory of motivation and psychological growth written by one of the best known and most influential humanists. Concerned with total personality development rather than classroom motivation, the book includes a valuable discussion of self-actualizing individuals and Maslow's views on human nature and potentialities.

Stainback, William C. et al. *Establishing a Token Economy in the Classroom.* Columbus, Ohio: Charles E. Merrill, 1973. Explains in some detail how token economy programs can be implemented, and includes a concise summary of the literature on the subject.

Waller, Patricia, and Gaa, John. "Motivation in the Classroom." In Richard H. Coop and Kinnard White, eds. *Psychological Concepts in the Classroom.* New York: Harper and Row, 1974. Among the topics discussed in this article are modeling, goal-setting, the measurement of students' motives, "the hierarchy of needs" concept, and multiple determination of human behavior.

Weiner, Bernard. "Motivation." In Robert Ebel, ed. *Encyclopedia of Educational Research.* New York: Macmillan, 1969. Weiner's contribution to this valuable reference book includes a summary of research findings on a variety of problems in the classroom motivation area.

9

Factors That Inhibit Learning

At the beginning of the last chapter, as you may recall, we noted that of the various factors that affect human learning none is more crucial than the individual's motivation and his ability to learn. The term *ability to learn* ordinarily implies intelligence; in fact, intelligence is commonly defined as the ability to learn. But in addition to the mental abilities implied by the word *intelligence*, there are also physical and emotional factors that have a bearing on how much and how well a person learns.

Serious deficiencies in either the mental, physical, or emotional order constitute what are referred to as learning disabilities. While these so-called disabilities might not literally render a person incapable of learning, they do tend to inhibit his learning. They are also likely to have a debilitating effect on the individual's motivation toward learning. In this chapter we shall discuss first some mental factors, and then some of the physical and emotional factors, that cause—or at least contribute to—difficulties with classroom learning.

MENTAL FACTORS

Just about every teacher in any class at any age or grade level soon comes to recognize, if only through casual observation, that some of his students are slower, or duller, or less gifted intellectually than others. For some students, a single explanation of the material is all that is necessary. "You tell them once, and they've got it." Others might have to have the explanation repeated two or three times before they understand. Some need no explanation at all. They have already learned the material that is being taught, they can figure things out for themselves and discover whatever it is the teacher would like them to learn, or they are bright enough to keep one step ahead of the teacher and several steps ahead of their classmates. And then there are those who just cannot seem to "get it" no matter what the teacher does. Depending on the degree of their mental subnormality, these might be classified as either slow learners or mentally retarded.

SLOW LEARNERS

The term slow learner is commonly used with reference to children with IQs between about 80 and 90. Approximately 15% of the population falls within this range. The 80 to 90 IQ range is, of course, purely arbitrary. For all practical purposes, there is no difference whatsoever between children with IQs of, say, 79 and 81, or 88 and 93. Differences of five or six points in IQ could easily result from some sort of testing error, and there is nothing inherently special about 80 or 90.

As we shall see later in this chapter, both the whole concept of the IQ and the tests from which IQ scores are derived have not only been questioned and criticized, but vigorously denounced. Certainly they have been misunderstood and misused. But before trying to clear up some of these misconceptions, let's see how IQs have been used to differentiate "slow learners" from those who are "normal" or above average on the one hand, and "retarded" on the other

Those with IQs of 90 or above are considered to be within the normal or above average range. Ordinarily they have the ability to get along fairly well in a regular classroom without much special help. Those with IQs below 75 or 80, on the other hand, are usually classified as retarded or mentally deficient. They need a great deal of special help. In between, the child we are calling a slow learner is one who is by no means retarded or in need of "special education," but is likely to need some extra help in a regular classroom. He is capable of learning just about anything that the average child is capable of; it just takes him longer.

Students who are slow in learning one subject are frequently slow in learning others. But this is not always the case. It is not exactly common, but neither is it uncommon, to find a child who is slow in learning how to read, for example, but is average or above in learning, say, mathematics. One reason for this phenomenon is that different abilities are required for learning different subjects. Whatever a person's IQ might be, he is likely to have more verbal than numerical ability, or vice versa. These different abilities are not always clearly indicated by his IQ. We should also recognize that a child who is slow in mastering the standard academic curriculum might be quite talented in music or art, for

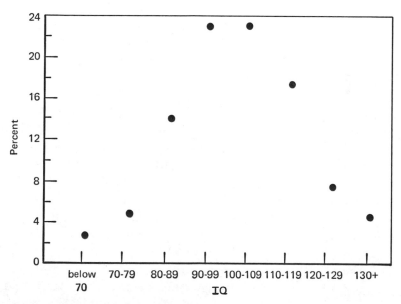

The Approximate Percentage of Individuals
Throughout the Country at Various IQ Levels

example, or very quick to learn skills that depend on manual dexterity or spatial visualization or a kind of common sense that again does not show up in his IQ.

HELPING THE SLOW LEARNER

In teaching a slow learner, you need perhaps more than anything else a great deal of patience. You should not write him off as hopeless or incapable of learning. But neither should you expect him to keep up with children of average or above average ability. You will probably have to repeat your instructions and directions to him several times and in simpler words than those you would use with the other students. You will probably have to give him a lot more in the way of practice, drill, and review. You should introduce new material in small, easy steps, relating it to what he already knows and making your presentation as concrete as possible. Ordinarily, a programmed rather than an independent discovery approach is likely to be more effective, and short-range incentives more productive than reliance on his intrinsic motivation toward long-range goals.

One of the things you should guard against is having the slow learner become discouraged to the point of simply accepting failure as his lot in life. You should start him off with easy tasks, tasks with which he is all but certain to succeed, and see to it that his little successes are rewarded. You should try to discover and capitalize on his interests and his strong points, and be careful not to criticize him for his intellectual shortcomings or his slowness. You should not place him in competitive situations where he has practically no chance of winning and should focus a great deal of your efforts on building up his self-confidence.

Whether or not slow learners should be taught separately from average or above average students is a problem on which opinions differ. We shall examine the pros and cons of ability grouping as well as some other means of helping the slow learner proceed at his own rate through the regular course of study in the next chapter.

MENTAL RETARDATION

There are some real dangers in labeling people slow learners or retarded, especially when such labels are based only on the flimsy evidence of one's IQ. IQs simply are not that precise. If properly understood, however, these labels can serve a useful purpose by facilitating communication, if nothing else. Individuals with IQs below 80 are commonly classified as retarded, but a distinction is frequently made between three levels of retardation.

Those with IQs between 50 or 55 to 75 or 80 are referred to as educable. As an adult, an educable retarded person has a mental age of about 10. This means, roughly, that he is capable of learning academic material up to about the fifth grade level, but it is likely to take him several years longer than the average 10-year-old to attain that level. Given the necessary special help, these individuals can be taught the fundamental school subjects as well as other useful skills. They can become, and many have become, responsible, self-supporting members of society, hardly distinguishable from "normal" people.

Just as there is no sharp line that separates normal students from slow learners, or slow learners from educable retarded individuals, so is there no exact point on an IQ scale that clearly distinguishes educable from trainable retarded people. But trainable retardation implies an IQ of about 20 to 45 or 50. As an adult, the trainable person has a mental age of 6 or 7. The implication is that he can be trained, but not educated. He is able to take care of himself physically, to communicate orally, and might be able to perform a number of useful tasks that do not require a great deal of intellectual prowess. Those with IQs below 20 or 25 are classified as custodial retarded. Having a mental age of about 2 or 3, these individuals are almost completely dependent upon others for the satisfaction of even their simplest personal needs. If their families are unable to take care of them, as is frequently the case, they need to be raised in special institutions.

A great deal of important work has been done in recent years with respect to helping retarded children and adults, including those who are classified as custodial. Some of the previously discussed principles of behavior modification seem to be particularly promising in this regard. The whole field of Special

Education, along with the related area of Learning Disabilities, has become one of the most challenging and productive fields in all of education. Since this book is intended for the "regular" teacher rather than the specialist, I shall forego any further discussion of retarded individuals and focus on the difference in mental abilities that are to be found in "regular" classrooms. More specifically, I should like to consider the concept of intelligence.

INTELLIGENCE

Individuals undoubtedly differ from one another in something called intelligence. But what is intelligence? Ask ten different psychologists and you are likely to get ten different answers. Many definitions of intelligence are available, but none of them is universally accepted or perfectly satisfactory. In this respect, the word *intelligence* is like other abstract terms such as life, love, beauty, truth, health, etc., which do not lend themselves to neat, concise definitions. To avoid the difficulty of trying to define intelligence, I am going to avoid using that word for a while and will use instead the term scholastic aptitude. This is why.

Psychologists are in general agreement that whatever intelligence is, it is not a single, global, unitary, general ability. It is rather a name for several different, relatively independent abilities. Please note the plural: abilities. As I see it, there is, strictly speaking, no such thing as intelligence so it is futile to try to define it. Intelligence, in the final analysis, is just a word, a name, an arbitrary symbol, a blanket term to designate many different kinds of mental abilities. Those mental abilities which are necessary or relatively important for scholastic achievement constitute scholastic aptitude, just as those abilities which are necessary for success in the fields of music or mechanics constitute musical or mechanical aptitude.

Every person has, in varying degrees, several mental abilities. Psychologists do not agree on the exact number and nature of these abilities, but whatever their nature or number, so-called intelligence tests do not measure or even purport to measure all of them. Since there are literally hundreds of mental ability tests available, each one at least a bit different from every other one,

I have to speak generally. Generally speaking, these tests—whether they are called intelligence tests, mental ability tests, or scholastic aptitude tests—measure the kinds of abilities necessary for, or correlated with, scholastic success in a traditional, academic curriculum. They measure a person's abilities to use and understand words, to compute arithmetically, and to manipulate numbers, to perceive similarities and differences, to do abstract logical reasoning, to remember and to solve problems requiring spatial visualization or convergent thinking.

Ordinarily, these kinds of tests do not measure or attempt to measure a person's creative or divergent thinking abilities. They do not measure his critical thinking abilities, his abilities to solve practical problems that he might encounter outside the school, or his abilities to cope with his environment. They do not measure his social intelligence, that is, his abilities to get along with, influence and lead other people. They do not measure his common sense; they do not indicate whether he has the intelligence to come in out of the rain.

Thus, it is possible (though not necessarily probable) that a person can have a high IQ and a great deal of scholastic aptitude without having very much of some of these other kinds of mental abilities. Similarly, a person can have a low IQ, a small degree of

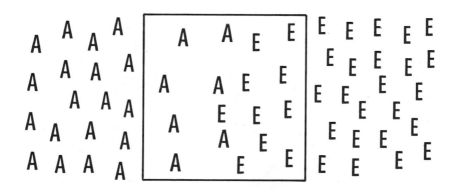

The A's represent a person's mental abilities (or aptitudes), the E's the effects of his environment (or his experiences), and the box an intelligence test. The test measures *some* of his As and reflects *some* of his E's, but *not all* of them.

197

scholastic aptitude, but be average or above in creativity, practical problem solving abilities, etc. In either case, the individual is more "intelligent" in some respects than others. For educational purposes, we are particularly concerned with the kinds of intelligence (or the mental abilities) necessary for scholastic achievement.

APTITUDE AND ACHIEVEMENT

At this point we might recognize the distinction that is commonly made between aptitude and achievement. Aptitude refers to a person's ability to do something. Achievement pertains to what he has already done. You might have a great deal of aptitude for playing the piano or repairing automobiles or for learning foreign languages, for example, even though you have never actually learned how to do these things. If you have achieved in these areas, however, it is obvious that you have or had the requisite abilities. It is much easier to infer aptitude from achievement than it is to predict achievement on the basis of presumed aptitude.

Tests of scholastic achievement measure the knowledge that a person has acquired in some particular subject area. They measure what or how much a person has learned about history, for example, or mathematics, or how well he has learned to read. Tests of scholastic aptitude do not primarily attempt to measure what the individual has learned, but his ability for future learning. They are used to estimate how much or how quickly the individual is capable of learning. They are used to predict scholastic achievement in the months or years ahead, to give teachers, school administrators, and others some indication of what to expect of that individual.

As predictors of scholastic achievement, tests of scholastic aptitude are roughly about as accurate as weather forecasts, public opinion polls predicting election outcomes, economists' predictions about what the stock market will do next month, or computers predicting the outcome of a football game.

Scholastic aptitude tests, as we have seen, do not measure all of a person's mental abilities; they only measure some of them. Moreover, the abilities that they do measure or try to measure are not measured perfectly or directly. In most cases there is a fairly high correlation between one's IQ and his scholastic success. Usually, the higher a person's IQ, the higher the grades he receives. Usually, but not always.

Aptitude is only one factor that affects achievement. The student's motivation, his attitudes, his physical and mental health, the encouragement he receives or does not receive, etc., might be just as important and possibly more important than his IQ, provided that his IQ is not too low or too high. Students with IQs much below 90 rarely do outstanding schoolwork and it is a mistake to expect it. If highly motivated, given more time and extra help, they might do good work, but it is not likely that they will do the excellent work of which a 130 IQ child is capable. As for the 130 IQ child, while he has the ability to achieve very highly, there is no guarantee that he will apply himself and use that ability. He might decide to be an underachiever.

INTELLIGENCE QUOTIENTS: HELP OR HINDRANCE?

In the preceding pages, I have made rather extensive use of the term IQ. I have also made a number of references to the so-called intelligence tests, or tests of scholastic aptitude, from which they are derived. Such tests, as has been noted, are not beyond criticism. Some educators and psychologists maintain that these tests are worse than useless, that they are positively harmful to students and to the cause of education, and that they should be done away with entirely. In some districts they have indeed been prohibited by law and can be used only in special cases.

The main objections to these tests is their alleged cultural bias. Minority group students typically score lower on these tests than middle-class children do. A common explanation of this differential is that the tests are unfair to or invalid for minority students because they have been standardized on and are intended for use with white middle-class children; that they use language and presume a background of experience which is inappropriate for those who are not white or middle class; and that they really do not measure intelligence—or even scholastic aptitude—so much as they reflect the individual's socioeconomic or cultural background. It has been argued that low test scores serve only to stigmatize the recipients, to categorize them unfavorably, and cause teachers as well as other school personnel to preconceive of them as slow learners or retarded or incapable of learning when in fact such is not the case at all.

A smaller number of educators and psychologists, on the other hand, regard these tests as extremely valuable. At least one prominent psychologist maintains that they are the greatest single practical contribution of psychology to education. At least a few teachers maintain the child's IQ is the most important single fact about a student that they would want to know or would need to know in order to help him.

It seems to me, as I believe it does to the majority of educators and psychologists, that tests of mental ability are neither as good as their proponents claim nor as bad as their critics make them out to be. Certainly these tests are not perfect, but what is? Certainly they have been misused, but what has not been?

USES AND MISUSES OF MENTAL TESTS

If these tests are used properly and if the scores are interpreted correctly, they can serve a number of useful educational purposes. They would seem to be especially important for slow learners, underachievers, and gifted students. If these students are to be given the special help they need, they must first be identified. While tests might not be absolutely essential for such purposes of identification and while their scores can sometimes be very misleading, they can be used to supplement the teacher's feelings or personal judgment.

In order to individualize education, to help each student develop his potentialities, it is necessary to know what their potentialities are. Teachers' impressions are not always adequate for this purpose. No one knows how many very bright, highly talented students have gone through schools bored and unchallenged with their talents going to waste simply because those talents were not recognized. No one knows either how many children have been scolded or otherwise punished for poor school work, or have been branded lazy, uncooperative or unmotivated, when they simply did not have the ability to keep up with the rest of the class or measure up to the teacher's expectations.

But no one knows either how many students have been unfairly and improperly labeled dumb, or slow, or stupid, or even retarded, and have had those labels follow them throughout their scholastic careers, prejudicing their teachers because somebody who should have known better did not. Test results can be and undoubtedly have been misused, misunderstood, and misinterpreted. But when this happens, the fault, it seems to me, rests not with the tests but with the people who misuse them.

INTERPRETING TEST SCORES

In interpreting "intelligence" test scores, and in trying to derive meaning from them, there are a number of points you should keep in mind. For one thing, it is quite possible for an individual to obtain different IQs on different tests. It is also quite possible for a person to obtain different IQs on the very same test taken at different times or under different circumstances. Moreover, while IQs tend to be fairly stable over a number of years, they can and do increase, not uncommonly up to 20 or more points, with the passing of time. Tests given to preschoolers or children in the primary grades are likely to bear little resemblance to those obtained at the high school level.

Do not forget that factors other than ability play an important part in scholastic achievement; that there is good reason to question the validity of "intelligence" tests when they are used with so-called disadvantaged or minority group students; that they measure only some, but not all, of a person's mental abilities; and that one's IQ does not by any means reveal the whole story of learning abilities or disabilities.

EFFECTS OF HEREDITY AND ENVIRONMENT

One of the most controversial issues in the entire area of psychology has had to do with the relative effects of heredity and environment on a person's "intelligence." Despite the tremendous amount of research that has been done on this subject, the issue remains unresolved. There are those such as Arthur Jensen who maintain that the amount of a person's intelligence is determined by his genes, and is thus fixed at the instant of his conception. Thereafter, little if anything can be done to increase the intellectual capacity with which he has been endowed. Others are of the opinion that one's intelligence is determined more by his environment, that it can and does change in accordance with the individual's training, experience, intellectual and sensory stimulation, and other external factors. Both the hereditarians and the environmentalists offer convincing evidence in support of their positions.

The most common view is that intelligence depends on neither heredity nor environment alone, but on the interaction of the two. Heredity seems to set certain limits within which a person is capable of developing intellectually, while the degree or extent to which he develops within those limits depends on the kind of environment in which he is raised. Thus, an individual with good heredity who is raised in a good environment will ordinarily be able to achieve more intellectually than one with a good heredity raised in a poor environment or one with a poor heredity raised in a good environment. In other words, such environmental factors as the quality of one's home or the school he attends or the other educational opportunities he has exerts different influences on different individuals depending on the inherited potentialities they have to begin with. Similarly, the same inherited potentialities can be expected to develop more fully in an intellectually stimulating environment than in one which is not so stimulating.

A MODERATE POSITION

There are two errors to be avoided in this respect. One is the extreme hereditarian view that some people are simply "born losers" intellectually, that they are "stuck with" relatively low degrees of mental ability, and that there is not much that anyone can do to alter that situation. The other is the extreme environmentalistic position that by appropriate forms of education or other kinds of human intervention, a person's alleged hereditary limitations can be overcome, and that just about anyone—barring some organic deficiency—can acquire a great deal more ability than he has at any given moment.

These extreme positions underlie two mistakes that have been made with respect to slow learners and educable retarded individuals. One is to dismiss them as hopeless, incapable of learning, or not even worth trying to teach. The other is to expect them to achieve standards that have been set for average or above average students.

Whether learning disabilities of a mental nature are due primarily to heredity or environment is a problem that at this moment we need not even try to settle once and for all. Whatever the source of these disabilities might be, they do exist. But whatever the degree of these disabilities might be, it is most unlikely that any individual uses the abilities that he does possess. Part of your job as a teacher, therefore, is to help develop your students' mental potentialities, be they great or small, to the fullest extent possible, and to try to gear your instructional program toward the needs of slow learners as well as average and gifted students. In the next chapter we shall discuss some means of doing these things. But next let's consider some other factors that inhibit learning.

PHYSICAL FACTORS

Physical factors that inhibit learning are likely to require specialized medical treatment. All I shall do in this section, therefore, is mention some symptoms of organic disorders that you should be able to recognize so as to make necessary referrals or at least appropriate allowances in your classroom.

GENERAL HEALTH

A student who is inattentive, unresponsive, or whose achievement leaves much to be desired is not necessarily unmotivated toward or incapable of learning. He simply might not feel well, or he might have a fairly serious physical ailment that has thus far gone unnoticed. It would be beneficial if every child and adolescent periodically received a rather thorough physical examination, if he ate three well-balanced, nutritious meals a day, received plenty of sleep, and a lot of fresh air, sunshine and exercise. But many, of course, do not, and their school work suffers.

Particularly at the elementary school level, teachers whose pupils frequently complain of headaches, for example, or upset stomachs, dizziness, or various aches and pains, or who have to make many more trips than usual to the lavatory, or who experience nausea, or appear to be very tired or overweight should bring these matters to the attention of the school nurse, if there is one, or to the child's parent if there is not.

SENSORY IMPAIRMENTS

Students are sometimes branded slow learners, or behavior problems, or even retarded simply because of some undetected visual or auditory defect that prevents them from keeping up with the rest of the class. Their only problem might be that they cannot see or hear as well as the others.

You should bring the matter to the attention of the students' parents if any of the following are observed: If you notice a student holding a book very close to his eyes, leaning forward or tilting his head in order to see the board or something you are demonstrating, rubbing his eyes as though to brush away a blur, attempting to brush off specks of dirt or something else that he "sees" on his paper, or stumbling over objects that are not directly in his line of vision; or if you observe that he is constantly frowning, squinting, blinking, or that his eyes are usually red or watering.

Similarly, if you notice that a student regularly fails to respond when called upon to recite, if he turns his head to one side or cups his ear as though straining to hear, if he frequently asks to have information repeated, if he appears to be inattentive and off in a world of his own, if he does not carry out instructions properly, if he shows little or no interest in group discussions and rarely participates in them, you might have reason to believe that he has a hearing problem that is interfering with this learning.

HYPERKINESIS AND HYPOKINESIS

Two other ways in which physical factors have an adverse effect on learning are referred to as hyperkinesis and hypokinesis. Hyperkinesis is the name given to the behavior of a person who is "constantly" in motion or "excessively" active. The hyperkinetic individual is always on the go. He cannot sit still. He is always fidgeting, leaving his seat, turning around, touching things, and seems to be "into" everything. He cannot seem to control his "nervous energy" and it might tire you just to watch him for a while. The hypokinetic individual is just the opposite: slow, dull, listless, apathetic, disinterested, timid, and generally inactive with respect to motor behavior.

There is no one precise point on a scale where "normal" activity can be clearly distinguished from that which is "hyper" or "hypo." The difference is essentially one of degree and cause. There is no particular advantage to labeling a person hyperkinetic or hypokinetic, but if his behavior does seem to deviate significantly from that of the others in his class along these lines, it might indicate that he is more in need of medical attention than, say, scolding.

The organic causes of hyperkinesis or hypokinesis are not known for sure, but they seem to be related to endocrine imbalance in the glandular system or to certain chemical processes within the brain or central nervous system. Drugs have been found to be effective in alleviating the symptoms of these disorders, but their use is by no means universally recommended. At any rate, the diagnosis and treatment of children who are excessively active or abnormally inactive should be left to specialists.

OTHER DISABILITIES

Authorities in the field of Special Education have identified dozens of other learning disabilities that are at least partly rooted in the individual's physiological condition. Some of these are very specific and highly technical in nature often involving perceptual-motor difficulties. Impairments in "laterality," for example, refers to the individual's preferential use of only one eye or hand or other part of the body. Impairments in "directionality" refers to his inability to follow directions involving left-to-right or top-to-bottom movements of the eye, hand, etc.

One of the most common of all learning disabilities is called dyslexia. The word dyslexia simply means the inability to read. Since reading is so basic to classroom learning, the terms dyslexia and learning disabilities are sometimes used interchangeably. More specifically, dyslexia refers to the difficulty some children (and adults) have in distinguishing between two letters, such as b and d, or between two similar printed words, such as who and why. In short, it refers to the inability to translate written symbols into sounds, or sounds into meaning. This, of course, is what reading is all about.

With respect to dyslexia or other kinds of learning disabilities, it is not always possible to clearly distinguish the mental from the physical, or the physical from the emotional factors that are involved. But let's move on to a consideration of situations where the emotional factor seems to be dominant.

EMOTIONAL FACTORS

Most students have the necessary ability to learn, are free of serious sensory defects, and are in reasonably good physical health. But what about their mental health? Mental health problems are generally regarded as one of the major factors that not only inhibit learning, but militate against motivation toward scholastic achievement as well.

MENTAL HEALTH

The term mental health might be somewhat misleading. While the word *mental* implies cognitive or intellectual processes, mental health refers more to one's emotional well-being or his personal and social adjustment.

A mentally healthy person is usually thought of as one who has, among other things, a favorable self-concept and a sense of personal worth. She is reasonably well satisfied with respect to her needs for safety, love, esteem, and self-fulfillment. She is relatively free of frustration, tension, anxieties, conflicts, feelings of inferiority, guilt, hostility, etc. Notice that I said "relatively" free. No one is perfectly free of these negative feelings, nor are any of an individual's needs ever completely and permanently satisfied. Thus, no one has perfect mental health. No one is completely free of personal, social, or emotional problems. The ability to solve such problems—or at least to learn to live with them—is, however, a necessary prerequisite for optimum scholastic achievement.

Here, for example, is a student who feels that he is unwanted, not needed, not loved. He feels that he is somehow not as good as others. Perhaps he hates other people, or fears them. At any rate, he is very insecure about what the future holds for him. This type of student cannot reasonably be expected to concentrate on the subject matter he is expected to learn. It is not likely that he will hang on his teacher's every word, or perform as well as he is intellectually and physically capable of performing. His attention, as well as his efforts, are more likely to be focused on trying to find ways of satisfying his needs, alleviating his anxieties, or escaping from the unpleasant emotional situation in which he finds himself. The type of individual I have in mind is not, in any meaningful sense of the word, mentally ill, nor should he be labeled "disturbed" or "maladjusted." But he does have unresolved personal problems that stand in the way of his scholastic success.

SYMPTOMATIC BEHAVIOR

There are many forms of behavior that might be symptomatic of emotional problems serious enough to constitute learning disabilities. Take, for example, something like thumb-sucking or nail-biting. In and of themselves, these behaviors do not inhibit learning. But they might be indicative of underlying strain, pressures, worries, or tensions that do. The same is even more likely to be true of fighting, bullying, verbal cruelty, or of timidity, suspicion, depression, and physical or psychological withdrawal. Though behaviors such as these do not directly prevent a person from learning, they might be manifestations of inferiority feelings, or feelings of hostility, or of some other emotional condition within the individual that have this effect.

Please note the use of the word "might" in the preceding paragraph. Certain forms of behavior might be symptomatic, might be indicative, might be manifestations of emotional problems. But then again they might not be. Some of the behaviors I have mentioned, and others that I will mention, might be quite normal for the individual at his stage of development. They might be no cause for concern, no serious impediment to learning or to good general mental health. When they occur with a high degree of frequency and intensity, however, and particularly when several of these behaviors occur together, they should be perceived as signs of some existing psychological problem with which the individual needs help. Let me simply mention some other behaviors that fall into this category:

> Underachievement, or a sudden deterioration in the quality of the student's work.
>
> Sensitivity to criticism and either crying or flying into a rage when corrected.
>
> Jealousy, the resentment of the happiness or success of others, or delight in their misfortunes.
>
> Extreme variations in mood from day to day, or from moment to moment.
>
> A low degree of frustration tolerance, expecting or demanding immediate gratification of one's desires.
>
> Tattling or lying in order to get someone else into trouble or to make oneself look good by comparison.
>
> Complaining of physical illnesses when medical examinations indicate that no illness exists.
>
> General unfriendliness or unsociability and poor peer group relations.

Excessive day dreaming, staring off into space.

Perfectionism or a compulsion to be the first and best in every-thing.

An unwillingness to try anything new or different.

An apparent inability to control one's own behavior.

Recklessness or lack of concern for one's own safety or the wel-fare of others.

Tendencies to either exaggerate or minimize one's accomplish-ments or his failures and limitations.

UNDERLYING FEELINGS

Underlying or accompanying most, if not all, of these behaviors are feelings of inferiority, insecurity, personal worthlessness, hostility, guilt, etc. But what are the origins of these so-called self-destructive feelings? To say that Matthew cannot (or will not) learn because he is "hostile" or feels "inadequate" is of little help to Matthew or his teacher or anyone else. The question remains: Why does he feel hostile or guilty or depressed or whatever?

There are several possible explanations, none of which is necessarily correct. Perhaps he has been subjected to excessive pressures to achieve well in school, in sports, or in some other activity. Perhaps his parents have expectations that for him are simply unrealistic. Perhaps he has been scolded, condemned, ridiculed, or humiliated for his failures to measure up to parental expectations. Perhaps he has been frequently and unfavorably compared with his brothers or sisters, his parents, the neighbors' children, or someone else. Perhaps his parents have inadvertently, if not explicitly, made him feel that they do not care what becomes of him. Perhaps, on the other hand, they have coddled and pampered him and overprotected him to the extent that he is now unable to cope with the demands of reality outside his home.

There are a number of other possibilities. Perhaps, as a Freu-dian would suggest, the roots of his problem go back to some traumatic experience in early childhood which now lies buried deeply in his subconscious and can only be brought to consciousness through psychoanalysis. Perhaps, as a behaviorist would suggest, the sources of his problem are to be found in his environment: in the pressures and strains, the demands and expectations of contemporary society; in the prevailing economic, social, political, and moral conditions of his community, his country, and his world.

Perhaps, as a phenomenologist might suggest, the heart of the problem lies, not "out there" in the physical environment, but within the individual himself, and his perceptions of himself and the world around him here and now. Perhaps the "real" cause of Matthew's behavior or of his self-destructive feelings will never be known "for sure." But fortunately for him the root causes need not be known with certainty in order for him to receive the help he needs in overcoming his problems or in learning to live with them.

SUGGESTIONS FOR HELPING

So here you are, teaching a class, and a couple of your Matthews and Susies are having a hard time keeping up with your other students because of what you believe are their emotional problems. Now what? Nobody expects you to psychoanalyze them, and I hope you will not try. Nobody expects you to go out and reform their environments, or their families, overnight, and I hope you will not try that either. But you can, of course, begin by having a talk with these individuals and later perhaps with their parents, or you might refer them to the counselor or school psychologist.

Within your own classroom you can demonstrate to all of your students—but perhaps in a special way to your Matthews and Susies—that you like them, that you care about them, that you are willing to listen to them. You can indicate that you understand them and that you are willing to try to help them. You can make a special effort so that you do not contribute to or intensify their feelings of anxiety, insecurity, etc. You can try to arrange conditions so that all of your students, but especially those with special needs, have a chance to experience success, develop self-confidence

210

and a feeling of personal worth. You can help them satisfy their needs for recognition and affiliation. You can do a lot of other "little things," most of which you will have to discover for yourself.

Throughout this section we have been primarily concerned with the effects of mental health on learning. But let's not overlook the reverse, that is, the effects of learning on mental health. One way of helping a person develop a favorable self-concept, a feeling of personal worth, and some of the other attributes associated with good mental health is to help him accomplish something that he regards as worthwhile. Scholastic achievement can be such an accomplishment. I am not suggesting, of course, that teaching Matthew how to read is automatically going to take care of all his personal, social, and emotional problems. But helping him learn to read, or teaching him in such a way that he will succeed in your biology class, might be the most important single contribution that you, as a teacher, can make to his overall development.

SUMMARY

Among the major factors affecting the quality of a student's learning are his mental abilities, physical condition, and emotional health. Deficiencies or disorders in these areas are likely to inhibit learning and, if serious enough, to render him incapable of learning in a regular classroom situation.

There are some real dangers in labeling students "slow learners" or "retarded" or as having "learning disabilities" particularly when these labels are based on the questionable evidence of his IQ alone. Some educators and psychologists maintain that IQs and the tests from which they are derived do more harm than good by prejudging and stigmatizing students with respect to their learning abilities and contribute to the formation of pessimistic self-fulfilling prophecies. Others maintain that, despite their shortcomings, if intelligence tests (or as they are more appropriately called tests of scholastic aptitude) are properly used and correctly interpreted, they can serve to help identify those with special educational problems and needs.

211

In interpreting IQs, we should keep in mind, among other things, the distinct possibility of cultural bias in intelligence tests, their lack of perfect reliability, the fact that they do not even attempt to measure all mental abilities, and that factors other than IQ enter into scholastic success. We should also recognize the needs and means of helping "slow learners" in a regular classroom, and not confuse them with underachievers or with individuals who are, strictly speaking, "retarded."

Authorities in the field of special education have identified dozens of learning disabilities that are at least partly physiological in nature. Other factors that inhibit learning are primarily emotional and concern the student's mental health.

Such behaviors as aggression, withdrawal, underachievement, and depression, for example, might be symptomatic of an emotional problem that requires the specialized attention of a counselor or school psychologist. Within his own classroom, however, a teacher is often in a position to help his students develop such positive traits as self-confidence, a feeling of personal worth, and a favorable self-concept. He can also make a special effort to do nothing that would be likely to contribute to, or intensify, their feelings of anxiety, inferiority, hostility, etc.

Recommended Readings

Combs, Arthur W. et al. *Helping Relationships.* Boston: Allyn and Bacon, 1971. Especially relevant to the section of this chapter dealing with emotional factors that affect learning. Explains from the standpoint of humanistic psychology what teachers can and should do to help students in this respect.

Forness, Steven R. "Implications of Recent Trends in Educational Labeling." *Journal of Learning Disabilities.* August/September, 1974. A short article describing the trend away from categorical labeling toward the identification of particular needs as a means of helping students with learning disabilities.

Gallagher, James J. "Phenomenal Growth and New Problems Characterize Special Education." *Phi Delta Kappan.* April, 1974. Reviews major trends and new techniques in the rapidly growing area of special education. Nineteen other articles in the same issue of this magazine focus on particular aspects of special education. A good introduction to the field.

Jensen, Arthur. "How Much Can We Boost IQ and Scholastic Achievement?" *Harvard Educational Review,* Winter, 1969. The controversial article in which the author sets forth his thesis that intelligence depends primarily on heredity. For a more detailed statement of his position, see his *Educability and Group Differences,* Harper and Row, 1973. For a series of seven articles highly critical of his position, see the *Harvard Educational Review,* Spring, 1969.

Kirk, Samuel A., and McCarthy, Jeanne, eds. *Learning Disabilities.* Boston: Houghton Mifflin, 1975. A collection of articles, some of them rather technical, dealing with a variety of problems and approaches in the area. Also recommended is Kirk's *Educating Exceptional Children,* 2d ed., Houghton Mifflin, 1972, which discusses the education of gifted as well as retarded children, and those with speech, hearing, visual, and other kinds of handicaps.

Menacker, Julius, and Pollack, Erwin, eds. *Emerging Educational Issues.* Boston: Little, Brown, 1974. Chapter 4, "Conflicts over Genetic and Environmental Determinants of Intelligence," includes five articles, each reflecting a different viewpoint on this controversial and very complex subject.

Psychology Today, September, 1972. This issue includes four short articles which are highly critical of methods of determining IQs and intelligence testing: "Abuse," "The Conspiracy," "The Lethal Label," and "Racial Gap."

Ringness, Thomas A. *The Affective Domain in Education.* Boston: Little, Brown, 1975. Discusses the nature and importance of affective education, as well as behavioral and humanistic principles for helping students in this area.

Samuda, Ronald J. *Psychological Testing of American Minorities.* New York: Dodd, Mead, 1975. Includes a good summary of the arguments pro and con testing and of the heredity-environment controversy. Also discusses the technical problems in attempting to measure intelligence, and environmental factors that influence test performance.

10

The Individualization
of Learning

The most important single variable in the learning process is the individual learner. The most important single principle in psychology is that no two individual learners are identical. These are hardly new discoveries or startling revelations, but they do point up what many educators perceive as one of their most challenging problems: the individualization of instruction.

Besides differing among themselves physically, intellectually, socially, and emotionally, students at every age and grade level differ, sometimes widely, in their interests and attitudes, their values and their goals, their special talents and their particular needs. They differ in their inherited potentialities and in the kinds of environments in which they have been raised. They differ with respect to their racial, national, cultural, socioeconomic, and particular family backgrounds, and in the varieties of previous experiences which they have consequently accumulated. In short, even within a particular classroom students differ not only in their abilities to learn and in what they already have learned, but they are also likely to differ in what they want to learn and maybe even in what they need to learn.

COGNITIVE STYLES

In addition to these rather obvious and well-known differences, students differ in another way which, for our present purposes, might be considered the most significant of all. They differ in what has been called their "cognitive styles." That is, even apart from ability and motivation they differ in their manner or modes of acquiring, retaining and applying knowledge. They differ in the ways they approach a learning situation, in the ways they perceive and organize and relate their experiences, and in the ways they respond to particular methods of instruction.

I am sure that if you were to take a survey of your classmates, you would find that some prefer "straight lectures" and others class discussions. Some would indicate that they learn more from their own independent reading than they do from either lectures or discussions or any combination of the two. Some would tell you that they learn best when studying for an objective test. Others would claim that they learn more when preparing for an essay test. Still others would insist that they learn best of all when they are not threatened with any type of test at all.

At any grade level some students learn most effectively by being programmed in highly structured, well-organized, teacher centered classrooms. They seem to need clear, logical explanations, a great deal of drill and review, and almost constant teacher direction. Even with the same subject matter, others do better in a more informal kind of classroom where they are permitted and encouraged to explore, discover, follow through on their own interests, use their own initiative, think for themselves, and reach their own conclusions.

These differences in cognitive style are due in part to the individual's abilities, in part to his personality, in part to his previous patterns of success or failure in learning, and in part to a number of other factors some of which might not as yet be fully understood or appreciated. But whatever the reason might be,

216

some students learn best through imitation. Others do better through trial and error. Some need a great many concrete examples of the concept of principle to be learned. Others function better at a more abstract level. Some are quick to perceive relationships among concepts and to comprehend the broad outlines of a subject, but to forget the details. Others focus on the specifics and retain the details, but have difficulty in putting them all together.

For reasons such as these, there is no one best way of teaching, nor can there be. What we might call good or effective teaching is always relative to the cognitive styles of particular students and the many other characteristics that distinguish one from another. This is why one of the perennial problems of education has been to find ways of instructing individuals as individuals. But as we shall see there is not any one best way of individualizing instruction either.

COMMON NEEDS AND TRAITS

Before we examine some of the means that have been employed to help individualize instruction, let's take a closer look at the concept of individuality as it relates to some of the other problems in the area of learning. Despite the fact that human beings do differ from one another, sometimes significantly, in just about every way imaginable, let's not lose sight of the fact that in some important respects, human beings are more alike than different. The implications of these human similarities for education are at least as great as those of the differences that separate us.

All human beings, for example, regardless of age, sex, race, IQ, cognitive style or anything else have the same general needs for love, respect, attention, approval, physical safety, self-fulfillment, a favorable self-concept, etc. All human beings, in other words, are motivated by the same kinds of drives toward the same kinds of goals simply because they are human beings.

Depending on their individual characteristics, backgrounds, and circumstances, different people perceive these goals and try to satisfy their needs in different ways. And that is important. But the differences between young people and old people, male people

217

and female people, white people and black people, poor people and rich people, smart people and not-so-smart people should not be allowed to obscure whatever it is that qualifies us for membership in the human race and gives us all a common "human nature."

In dealing with children and young people, it is well and good to keep in mind the many important differences among them. Maybe, as a teacher, you would like to get to know, and know well, each of your students as an individual. But maybe you have so many individuals in your classes that you cannot get to know any one of them very well. Maybe you would like to individualize your classes in some way or other but circumstances beyond your control prevent you from doing so. Cheer up. All is not lost. Casual observation and experience, along with the study of child or adolescent psychology, will enable you to form generalizations that will apply to many or most, though not all, of your students and suggest some ways you can help them "all together."

In our culture, for example, most ten-year-old boys are in many respects pretty much alike. No two of them are identical. Some deviate considerably from the average. But in general, as any developmental psychology book will detail, most of them have attained approximately the same degree of physical, mental, and social maturity. Most of them are likely to share similar interests and have similar educational needs. By definition most of them are average. Generally speaking most of them can profit by approximately the same educational program as that used for and with any other group of ten-year-old children. But note the qualifiers, "generally speaking" and "approximately."

Let's take another example. If I were to tell you that I have a 13-year old niece, even though you have never met her and know absolutely nothing else about her except her age and sex, you could—I believe—tell me a great deal about her. It is possible, of course, that you might be wrong in certain specific details. But drawing on your knowledge of other 13-year-old girls, the odds are that you have a reasonably accurate idea of what she is like physically, socially, mentally, and emotionally simply because she is a 13-year-old girl. Admittedly, she might be a giant or a dwarf. She might be a genius or she might be seriously retarded mentally. But the odds are that she is not. The statistical probability is that she is in most respects very much like other girls her age and can

218

be instructed accordingly. Still, my niece is more than a statistical probability.

Pardon me if I am being repetitious or seem to be belaboring the obvious, but what I am trying to do is caution you against two mistakes. One is the view that "they" are all alike, that if you know one, you know them all. The other is that "they" are all so different from one another that it is impossible to make accurate generalizations about them. Whether "they" refers to 10-year-old boys, 13-year-old girls, "middle class" children, "disadvantaged" children, gifted students, slow learners or any other group, neither of those views is completely right or completely wrong.

With respect to the purposes and methods of education, there are two corresponding mistakes. One is that all students (excluding the seriously retarded or disturbed) can and should be expected to learn pretty much the same thing at the same time in the same way from the same teacher to the same degree. The other is that each individual student needs and has a right to a unique educational experience specifically geared to his particular interests, goals, talents, etc., with little or no concern for the needs or expectations of society and with little if any regard for what "others" are learning.

Certainly individual differences should be taken into account and considered seriously in the planning of each student's education. Certainly education should be very much concerned with helping each student actualize his particular potentialities and develop his particular individuality. But it is also important to remember that there are certain skills and certain bodies of knowledge that are practically essential for survival, to say nothing of success, in our society. Schools are established and maintained to help individuals learn this knowledge and acquire these skills whether they happen to feel like learning them or not. Thus, the problem under consideration involves finding viable, practical, realistic ways and means of instructing diverse students, but without exaggerating their differences or neglecting their common educational needs.

DEGREES OF INDIVIDUALIZATION

At this point I should like to make a rather fine distinction between two closely related concepts: "taking individual differences into account" and "individualizing instruction." The latter cannot be done without the former. The former, however, does not insure the latter. By and large our schools have done considerably more with "taking individual differences into account" than they have with "individualizing instruction."

The elective system, for example, is one way of taking into account and making some provision for difference among students' interests, abilities, vocational goals, etc. While some schools offer a broad array of courses from which the student is free to pick and choose cafeteria style, on the assumption that he knows what is best for him or that she should be permitted to satisfy her own personal tastes with a minimum of external regulation, other schools offer fewer and more restricted choices. But in either case, once a student elects a particular course, he is likely to be held to the same requirements as everyone else who chooses that course. Similarly, when homogeneous grouping or track systems are used as a vehicle for taking individual differences into account, once a student has been placed in a section with others of similar abilities, interests or needs, the differences among them that remain might be overlooked so that their programs are not "really" individualized at all.

The term individualization of instruction, like so many other terms in education and psychology, has no precise, universally accepted definition. But ordinarily it implies something more than simply recognizing individual differences or taking them "into account." It implies either administrative procedures or instructional strategies within a classroom designed to do something to help students on a one-to-one basis. The focus is on the particular student, not as a type, such as gifted, slow learner, underachiever or disadvantaged, but as a unique individual with a particular set of needs and a cognitive style of his own.

But even thus conceived, there are still widely varying degrees of what is called individualization to be found in our schools. Here is an English teacher, for example, who gives his students a choice of writing a report on any one of the novels by Charles Dickens. He claims to be individualizing, and perhaps he is. But here is another teacher who says, "Hell, that's not individualization. Individualization means letting the student report on any book that he wants to or, if he prefers, on no book at all."

Individualized programs have been designed to allow for

options of flexibility with respect to any one or combination of four variables: objectives, methods and materials, the degree to which the objectives are to be achieved, and the period of time within which they will be achieved. Thus, in one class each student might be permitted to decide for himself what he will learn about the subject and how well he will learn it. In another class, the teacher or the school administration establishes the objectives but allows each student to proceed at his own pace in achieving them. In one class the students are all expected to use the same textbooks or workbooks, but in different ways. In another, they can select their own instructional materials from a variety that are available to them. With the very same group in the very same room, a teacher might insist that every student achieve at least, say, 90% in spelling, while in art or social studies she simply encourages each to do his best, whatever his best might be.

But let's consider more specifically some of the procedures that are commonly used for the purpose of individualizing instruction or at least providing for differences among individual students in a manner that might facilitate individualization.

ABILITY GROUPING

The practice of grouping students on the basis of their ability or previous achievement in a particular subject certainly does not eliminate the differences among students in a particular classroom. But it does reduce the range of differences within the class. It also reduces the number of students in the class who require extraordinary help, and increases the prospects of their getting it. Nobody regards ability grouping as the final answer to the problem of individualization. But some teachers and school administrators are convinced that it is a step in the right direction as a practical means of helping both slow learners and exceptionally bright students. Others, however, believe that this practice is likely to do more harm than good.

Those who favor ability grouping believe that it is likely to be more challenging to the gifted student than work in a regular heterogeneous classroom would be, that he will not be held back by slower learning classmates, and that he will be stimulated by the presence in his class of others who are all about as bright and presumably interested as he. Proponents also claim that ability grouping enables slow learners to receive instruction geared directly toward their needs and relieves them of having to keep up with or be compared with more intellectually talented classmates.

Critics of ability grouping are fearful of the effects of that practice on the slow learner's self-concept when he finds out that he is in the "dumb" group. They also have some misgivings about the possibility of developing an unhealthy kind of vanity or feeling of superiority on the part of the "elite." Even more prevalent is the belief that ability grouping contributes to the so-called self-fulfilling prophecy, by which the teacher of the slow group does not expect much from her students, teaches them accordingly, and consequently "proves" that her predictions or expectations were valid. Perhaps the most commonly advanced argument against ability grouping is that slow learners learn more in a classroom with brighter children than they do when segregated, and that there are better ways of helping gifted students.

The arguments pro and con have gone on for a long time and will undoubtedly continue. Many teachers welcome the opportunity to teach a class full of bright or average students, but not nearly as many are eager to take on the slow groups. Temporary flexible subgrouping within a self-contained heterogeneous class is, of course, a viable alternative to separate classes or separate sections. Thus, the social and motivational benefits of heterogeneity are preserved, but children needing special consideration can receive it as part of a small subgroup when and as it is needed.

A tremendous amount of research has been done on ability grouping, but the results are contradictory and inconclusive. They seem to indicate that ability grouping in and of itself does not necessarily lead to greater scholastic achievement on the part of either slow or average or bright students, but neither is it detrimental to learning or to the learner's personality development. In and of itself, it just does not seem to make that much difference. Far more critical are the competence, personal characteristics, and intentions of the teachers and the methods and materials they employ. By reducing the range of mental differences within a class, ability grouping makes more individualized instruction possible, but it by no means guarantees it.

ACCELERATION AND ENRICHMENT

Instead of or in addition to ability grouping, the individual needs of brighter-than-average students can be met by means of some form of acceleration or enrichment. There are several ways of accelerating a student's progress through his educational program ranging from early entrance to kindergarten or the first grade (say, at age four) to advanced placement at the college level. In between, there are various possibilities for having a student skip a grade, combine two terms' work in one, or satisfy course requirements by studying on his own and then passing appropriate achievement tests.

As you might expect, there are those who object to acceleration mainly on the grounds of its possibly harmful effects on the individual's social development. But the available evidence, as opposed to opinion or theory, is far more favorable than unfavorable toward acceleration. Still, there are advantages to keeping the individual with others of approximately the same chronological age, which is why some educators prefer enrichment to acceleration as a means of helping the gifted.

Instead of rushing a bright third-grader, for example, directly into the fifth grade, it might be better to have him spend a year in the fourth—provided that he is given an opportunity to study more subjects at that level or that he is challenged to delve more deeply into the basic subjects. Certain so-called "enrichment experiences," such as field trips, visits to concerts, theatres, art galleries, etc., are of course of value to all students, not only the smart ones. The kinds of enriching experiences I have in mind are projects or assignments geared to the interests and abilities of brighter students as a substitute for at least part of the regular class work.

Thus conceived, enrichment comes closer to "real" individualization than ability grouping or acceleration, but no one of these excludes the other. Enrichment can be provided through independent research, differentiated assignments or some of the other strategies we will be considering shortly. But while the gifted child is being enriched or accelerated, what about his slower-learning cousin?

223

PROMOTION POLICIES

If a gifted child is permitted to skip a grade, should the slow learner be required to repeat a grade or a course until he has mastered its content? Even if school policies do not allow acceleration, should they encourage "social promotion" as a means of keeping the individual with others of his age? Should grade-to-grade promotion be automatic? Or should automatic promotion be outlawed? If one of your second graders has not learned second-grade material to your satisfaction, what should you do: pass him on to the third-grade teacher and let her worry about him next year, or retain the child yourself for another year and hope that he will mature enough for you to help bring him up to respectable second-grade standards?

Such questions have been frequently and sometimes emotionally debated and widely researched, but as yet they have no one single right or wrong answer. In general, research studies have tended to indicate that the advantages of promotion outweigh those of nonpromotion. So perhaps a good policy would be: when in doubt, give the student the benefit of the doubt and promote him. But there will probably be some doubt in every case about which course of action would be better for the child himself. So an even better policy would be to take into account as many relevant factors as possible, including the student's degree of slowness, the differences in his performance in various subject areas, his physical size and chronological age, his social relationships and his feeling of personal worth. But in the final analysis, the question centers around the teacher's judgment about the degree or probability that the student will profit from another year in the same grade if he is retained.

Research offers no hard evidence that requiring a child to repeat a grade will have "devastating" effects on his personality development or later scholastic achievement, as some advocates of a "no failure policy" have claimed. But neither is there any assurance that simply retaining the child and giving him nothing but more of the same will bring him up to par. In my opinion, automatic promotion policies make no sense whatsoever and are in conflict with the concept of individualization in that they systematically ignore significant human differences. But the idea of having a student repeat a grade year after year until he comes

224

up to "standards" does not make sense either. Hence, the need for a policy of deciding each case on an individual basis.

NONGRADED CLASSROOMS

Nongraded classroom arrangements enable each student to make "continuous progress" through the work of two or three grades without the need for agonizing decisions as to whether or not to promote, retain, or accelerate. In nongraded classrooms, there is no specified amount of material that every student must learn by a certain date in order to be promoted. There are, rather, sequential "levels of achievement" that must be attained before the individual is permitted to advance to the next higher level.

Ordinarily the levels that correspond to grades one through three, for example, can be completed in three years, but if a particular child needs more time he has it, and if he can accomplish the work in less time he is permitted to do so. Thus, there is no "failure" in the sense of a student's having to repeat a whole year's work because he did not come up to predetermined standards on schedule. Neither is there any need for the more capable student to wait for his slower learning classmates to catch up before he can proceed to more advanced work.

Although it has been tried at the high school and upper elementary levels, nongrading is most commonly used to replace what would ordinarily be the first three grades. The nongraded classroom is potentially an excellent vehicle for individualizing instruction by providing each student with an opportunity to progress at his own rate in each of the major subject areas. For example, a student might be working at one level in reading and a higher or lower level in mathematics.

The nongraded classrooms that have been found to be the most effective are managed by teachers who understand and are committed to its underlying philosophy. These teachers are well-organized and inclined to be highly structured, but are flexible, resourceful, and adaptable enough to provide individual assistance. They have available a wide variety of instructional materials as well as diagnostic and evaluative instruments to help ascertain and satisfy the educational needs of individual students. Not every

225

class that is labeled nongraded has such teachers or the diversity of tools necessary for "real" individualization.

SYSTEMATIC PROGRAMS

Simply placing a child in a nongraded classroom does not guarantee that he will learn anything of consequence or that his particular educational needs will be met. Neither does the practice of having him skip a grade or repeat a grade, or that of grouping him with others of like ability. All of these are potentially useful frameworks for individualization, but by itself none of these attacks the problem of individual differences as directly as possible. Something more than administrative regulations governing grade placement or grouping or promotions is necessary.

Some nongraded classes, as well as others that remain graded in the traditional manner, make use of rather systematic, formalized programs for individualization that have been developed locally to help their particular students. Other graded as well as nongraded classes have adopted even more highly systematic procedures that have been developed by outside experts for use throughout the country. The various locally developed programs differ from one another in operational detail as well as in principle. So do such nationally used programs as IGE, PLAN, and IPI, after which many local programs have been modeled.

IGE, Individually Guided Education, was developed at the University of Wisconsin in cooperation with the Kettering Foundation. Under this sytem, which is designed for use in elementary schools, teams of teachers along with the principal are responsible for planning and implementing individualized programs for students in their particular building. A variety of methodologies are employed, including independent study, tutoring, large group and small group instruction. IGE provides curriculum, evaluation, and other resource materials which local school personnel can adapt for their particular purposes.

PLAN, Program for Learning in Accordance with Needs, is a computer managed program conducted under the auspices of the Westinghouse Learning Corporation. The program can be used in grades one through twelve in the area of language, arts, mathematics, science, and social studies. Under PLAN each student works at his own rate with "teaching–learning units" that have been specifically designed for him. The student is free to select his own materials in order to achieve the behavioral objectives specified in his teaching–learning units, but much use is made of individually operated audiovisual equipment. Special tests are provided by PLAN to determine whether or to what extent the objectives have been achieved.

Let's look at the third of these systematic programs, IPI, somewhat more closely, not because it is necessarily better than IGE or PLAN, but just to give you a clearer idea of how one such program works.

INDIVIDUALLY PRESCRIBED INSTRUCTION

IPI, Individually Prescribed Instruction, programs were developed at the University of Pittsburgh for use in the first six or seven grades. IPI is based on the principles of programming and makes great use of behavioral objectives, both of which were discussed in Chapter 6. Under IPI there is no individualization with respect to the student's choice of objectives. The objectives are "prescribed" for him. But each student is able to work toward the prescribed outcomes at his own pace and moderately under his own direction.

As part of IPI, every student is given a series of placement tests at the beginning of the term to find out what he already knows about, or is able to do in, such basic subject areas as reading, mathematics, spelling, handwriting, and science. The results indicate the level at which he is ready to begin learning. Then he is given pretests for each unit of instruction within a subject area. After evaluating the results of these pretests, the teacher writes out an individualized prescription for each student much as a physician might do after giving a patient a physical examination. The prescription specifies what the student must do in order to achieve the objectives for that particular unit.

Each student is then given specially prepared worksheets or other self-instructing material geared to his specific prescription. For the most part, he is expected to work independently, but depending upon his particular needs, he might be temporarily assigned to a small group or given individual tutoring. The objectives of each prescription are stated in such a way that they can usually be achieved within a single class period. When a student is able to demonstrate mastery of the first unit, he is given a prescription for the second, and so forth.

Prescriptions are sequentially arranged from the simple to the more complex and are often cumulative in nature so that mastery of one is a prerequisite for success in the next. Mastery is arbitrarily defined as a score of at least 85% on the specially prepared tests. If a student does not achieve mastery, his particular errors and difficulties are noted and he is given the special help or remedial work he needs in order to overcome them.

IPI teachers do very little lecturing to the entire class. They spend most of their time administering tests, diagnosing individuals' needs, preparing the written prescriptions, evaluating students' progress, helping individuals on a one-to-one basis or instructing small groups of students who are experiencing the same particular difficulties. Ordinarily, a teacher is given special in-service training before he begins to work with IPI, and it is strongly recommended that he be given clerical or paraprofessional assistance with the vast amount of paper work that is involved.

The cost of IPI materials is not prohibitive, but the program does require a financial expenditure which some school districts might be unable to afford or unwilling to make. Thus, instead of purchasing IPI material, a number of ambitious and imaginative teachers have devised their own programs following the basic IPI principles or using ideas borrowed from other sources. Some of these do-it-yourself programs are, as you would expect, more elaborate than others and they have met with varying degrees of success. Among the systematic do-it-yourself approaches to the individualization of instruction are those involving the use of student-teacher contracts.

STUDENT-TEACHER CONTRACTS

Student-teacher contracts specify, usually in writing, what the student will do and what he will receive in return. Under this system, each student negotiates his own contract on an individual basis or selects one of several that the teacher offers as options. Thus, the student is permitted to choose (within limits) the objectives he will pursue.

As a teacher I might propose, for example, that if you read and write a report on ten books and twenty articles you will receive an *A* in the course, provided that your reports come up to minimum standards of acceptability which I will specify. I might suggest books and articles that I think would satisfy your particular interests and needs, but it will be your privilege (or responsibility) to select the material you will review. Maybe you think ten books and twenty articles is a bit much, so you propose that you report on two books and five articles and settle for a *B*. I do not think that this amount of work is worth more than a *C*, so we do some give-and-take bargaining until we come up with a contract the terms of which we both find reasonably satisfying.

With another student, I might recommend a different set of books or articles related more directly to her interests or needs. She might suggest oral rather than written reports. Another student might propose that instead of reports on reading, he do a type of field project that is more in line with his interests. Some of the students and I might agree that if they pass a test covering specified material with at least a score of, say, 75%, they will be assured of at least a *C* without doing anything else. If a student does not like to study for tests or write book reports or term papers or does not care for any of the other options I suggest, he is invited to devise an appropriate activity of his own. If he is not interested in grades, I might offer him a dozen token reinforcers or a gold star or a pizza and beer or whatever other type of incentive we can agree upon. The possibilities are endless.

Teacher-student contracts of the type under discussion are essentially variations of "differentiated assignments" which teachers have been giving for years; or of "independent study" programs, which have long been used at the college level and more recently but less frequently at the high school level; or of the time-honored practice of "extra work for extra credit."

Some form of contracting system can be used at any level from the kindergarten through the graduate school. It can be used either regularly or just occasionally in a regular classroom without any special materials, facilities, administrative readjustments, or financial expenditure (except perhaps for the beer and pizza). It can, moreover, take into account not only students' intellectual abilities, but differences in their interests, goals, backgrounds, etc. Like any other attempt at individualization, contracts have their drawbacks. One of them is that some students might feel that others are getting better "deals" than they are. But this is a possibility with any plan that attempts to treat different students differently. The alternative is to "treat them alike," but presumably this is precisely the practice that we are trying to get away from because "they" are not all alike.

AUTOMATED INSTRUCTION

Neither student-teacher contracts nor any of the other instructional strategies or administrative arrangements that we have discussed can be expected to solve the individualization-of-instruction problem alone. Neither can technology or any of the so-called self-instructing devices it has produced. But used along with some of these other procedures, automation has a potential for contributing significantly to the solution of the problem. This potential should not be overlooked.

Among the automated instructional devices I have in mind are such "tools" as teaching machines, programmed and scrambled textbooks, computer-assisted programs and closed circuit television, as well as films and film strips, tapes and records, and any other mechanical or electronic facility that a student can use on an individual basis. I refer to these as tools in the sense that I regard dictionaries, encyclopedias, blackboards, globes, pictures, and for that matter ordinary textbooks and workbooks as instruments that can be used to facilitate the learning process. I think it would be a mistake to rely exclusively on teaching machines, for example, just as it would be a mistake to rely exclusively on lectures or group discussions or textbooks. But I also think it would be a mistake to reject these machines on the grounds that they are, as has been charged, impersonal or dehumanizing.

Teaching machines vary considerably in cost, complexity, versatility, and effectiveness. They range from simple cardboard gadgets costing a couple of dollars to highly sophisticated electronic contrivances that run into the thousands of dollars. But automated instruction, as I have suggested, does not necessarily imply the use of any kind of machine. So simple a device as a stack of 3 in. X 5 in. index cards can be used for this purpose.

Suppose, for example, that you wanted to teach yourself (or someone else) Russian. On one side of each card you could write an English word and on the opposite side its Russian equivalent. You look at the English side, say, or better yet write down the Russian translation, and then flip the card over to receive your reinforcement. Then you reverse the process, beginning with the Russian words. Within a short period of time, you can acquire quite a vocabulary by this simple method of automation. But what about pronunciation and grammar? Well, for about $3.98 you can get an excellent set of records with an accompanying manual that might give you all the help you need.

If you need further information, you can always consult a Russian-English dictionary or a book on Russian grammar. If you want to know something about the history or culture or government of Russia, there are more books available on the subject than you could read in a lifetime. If you want to bring it all to life, you can view some of the fine film strips or movies that are available. Similarly you can teach yourself—and as a teacher you can help your students learn by and for themselves—a great many other subjects or skills by using commercially prepared self-instructing materials, or by producing your own.

With a wide variety of materials and equipment available; with the student being given a choice as to which of them he will use, or with a student being assigned to a particular program on the basis of his particular needs; and with each student allowed to proceed through a self-instruction program at his own rate without being pressured to keep up with the rest of his class, the possibilities of technology and automation for the individualization of instruction are practically unlimited.

TEAM TEACHING

Having paid our respects to technology, let's return to the human teacher. Just as students differ among themselves in their learning styles, as we noted at the beginning of this chapter, so do teachers differ in their styles of teaching. Some are at their best when

231

lecturing to a large audience. Others do better when explaining things to a small group, or in answering questions, or in working with individuals on a one-to-one basis. Some are better than others in conducting group discussions and have the knack of drawing students out. Some like to putter with gadgets; to others technology is anathema. Some are better than others with the paperwork aspects of teaching. They actually enjoy analyzing test scores, preparing records, filing reports, etc., and are good at that sort of thing. Others are not.

Some teachers cannot seem to function at all in anything but a business-like manner within a carefully organized, highly structured classroom environment. Others are more comfortable, and perform more effectively, in a more casual type of setting. Some thrive on routine; others prefer flexibility and spontaneity. Within a particular subject area, such as English, every teacher is likely to be more interested in some aspects of the subject, such as poetry or drama, than in others, such as grammar or composition. Yes, teachers differ among themselves much as students do.

Team teaching is not primarily intended as a means of individualizing instruction for the students, but as a way of providing for differences among teachers. The practice of having two or more (preferably more, say about four or five) teachers working together as a team can, nevertheless, be another useful instrument for individualization. If nothing else, team teaching increases the probability that a given student will encounter, at least for a while, a teacher whose style of teaching matches his style of learning. If one member of the team cannot help him, perhaps another one can.

There is no set formula for splitting up the responsibilities of the various members of a teaching team. But the theory behind the practice is that it allows teachers to specialize in or concentrate on a particular aspect of the total teaching process. One of these aspects might well be remedial work with individuals or small groups having particular kinds of difficulties. Another might be working with brighter students on enrichment type projects. Still another might be preparing self-instructional materials or working out a variation of something like IPI.

Like educational television, teaching machines, nongraded classrooms, "open" classrooms and other innovations of the last few decades, team teaching was for a while heralded as a kind of panacea. It has not turned out to be that at all. But like some other innovations as well as some old, established practices and procedures, it is one means of contributing to the solution of the problem under consideration.

PEER TUTORING

What about the practice of using some of the bright students as, in effect, members of a teaching team? Even apart from any concept of team teaching, what about having students tutor one another?

Fashions change in education as they do in so many other areas. Less than a hundred years ago, the one-room schoolhouse—which some historically-minded observers perceive as the forerunner of today's nongraded classrooms—was very much in vogue, and in some localities it still is, with one teacher instructing children between the ages of four or five to fifteen or sixteen on an individual basis. Commonly, the one-room schoolhouse teacher drafted into service one or some of the older, brighter students to help her teach the younger or slower ones.

Then education went through a phase when the one-room, nongraded classroom was regarded as unspeakably ineffective and pedagogically unsound. So, as a means of reducing the degree of differences among students in a particular room, someone hit on the idea of dividing them into grades, more or less on the basis of chronological age. Also viewed with disdain for a while was the practice of peer tutoring: "the students being tutored would get an inferiority complex, they would not learn the stuff right, it was not fair to make the brighter kids do the teacher's work," etc. The nongraded classroom of today, is, of course, a far cry from the one-room schoolhouse of the nineteenth century, and the kind of peer tutoring I have in mind is not the same as the older practice of using students as unpaid teacher's assistants. But the general idea of peer tutoring is once again back in style.

As I am sure you have noticed from your own experience, one of your fellow students can sometimes explain something that comes up in class more clearly than your professors can. Similarly at the elementary and high school levels students are likely to

233

perceive one another's learning problems, having recently experienced such problems themselves, and by speaking the same language can help their friends overcome those problems. The practice of matching up students so that one can coach the other has strong possibilities for giving the slower student the individual help and perhaps drill that he needs. At the same time, this practice can also be helpful to the student doing the tutoring. It fits in with the old adage that you never really know a subject until you have taught it, and that the best way to learn a subject is to try to teach it, or write a book about it.

OPEN CLASSROOMS

The final approach to the individualization of instruction that I will mention is some form of open classroom. I say "some form of" because so-called open classrooms are not all alike. Some are considerably more open—in the sense of allowing student freedom—than others. There is, then, no one set pattern that every open classroom can, or should try to, follow. To try to standardize or formalize the open classroom would defeat its very purpose and the assumptions which underlie it.

Ordinarily an open classroom is most readily distinguished by its physical appearance. The room is likely to be subdivided into several work areas, each equipped with a variety of instructional materials appropriate to a certain activity such as reading, science, mathematics, or art. The student is free to move from area to area using the materials to a certain extent as he chooses. He has the opportunity to help set his own individual objectives, and a large share of the responsibility for selecting the means of attaining them.

The teacher does very little in the way of teaching the whole class simultaneously. Rather, he acts as a kind of roving resource person, working with individuals or small groups on projects that they have undertaken. He might volunteer his assistance on occasion, but more likely will not intervene until asked. It is quite possible that at any given moment in an open classroom, no two students are engaged in precisely the same activity. They are certainly not all on the same page of the same workbook. But everyone is likely to be busy with some activity in which he is genuinely interested.

There is no specified material that has to be covered by a certain date, no across-the-board standards that everyone is expected to achieve. Individual student-teacher contracts might be used, but not necessarily so. There is, of course, a great reliance on intrinsic motivation and discovery learning. Great emphasis is also placed on creativity, self-expression, exploration, experimentation, and the cultivation of curiosity. Competition is minimized; cooperation encouraged. In short, the open classroom is characterized by informality, flexibility, spontaneity, diversity, and self-direction.

Although attempts have been made to extend the open classroom concept upward to the middle school, junior high and high school levels, it has been used most widely and successfully at the primary and early elementary levels.

Proponents claim that the open classroom not only provides for individual differences among students, but that it also helps them learn to learn on their own, gives them a chance to experience success, develops self-confidence and self-discipline, and makes learning an enjoyable experience. Critics and skeptics might be willing to concede some or even all of these points, but they wonder aloud whether the students can or will learn as much of the fundamental subject matter and basic skills under these conditions as they would in a more conventional teacher-directed classroom.

Thus far, there is no conclusive evidence I know of that proves unequivocally that the advantages (or disadvantages) of the open classroom are as great as its proponents (or detractors) claim. As is the case with any of the other attempts at individualization that have been mentioned, this approach in and of itself will not solve the problem to everyone's satisfaction. But it does seem to offer some good possiblities for helping with it.

SUMMARY

At any age or grade level, individual students differ from one another not only in their abilities to learn and in what they have previously learned, but in what they want to learn, in what they need to learn, in their styles of learning, and in a number of other significant dimensions. Thus it is unrealistic and ineffective, if not actually detrimental to their overall education, to expect every member of a class to learn the same thing to the same degree at the same time in the same way. Despite the individual characteristics that distinguish them from one another, most students of a given age have a number of needs and traits in common. Thus, a completely individualized instructional program might not be necessary or desirable, even if it were possible.

Most schools make some attempt to at least recognize and try to provide for differences among their students. Individualized programs have been designed for options or flexibility with respect to any one or combination of four variables: objectives, methods and materials, the degree to which objectives are to be achieved or mastered, and the amount of time students will be given in order to achieve them.

Among the more commonly used means of individualizing, or helping to individualize instruction, are some form of ability grouping, acceleration and enrichment, nonpromotion and non-graded classrooms or "continuous progress" plans. Other strategies include the use of specially designed systematic programs such as Individually Prescribed Instruction or Individually Guided Education, the use of student-teacher contracts, teaching machines, computers, programmed textbooks, self-instructing worksheets, and peer tutoring. Each of these has its uses and its limitations. Just as there is no one best way of teaching "in general," neither is there any one best way of individualizing instruction.

The problem is by no means new, but at no time in the history of education has a search for practical means of individualization had a higher priority. While no one means of individualizing instruction in and of itself can be expected to solve the problem to everyone's satisfaction, a combination of some of the strategies that have been mentioned—along with others which will be devised in the years ahead—can go a long way toward helping each student achieve a high quality education in his own way, at his own rate, and in terms of his own abilities and needs.

Recommended Readings

Block, James H. *Mastery Learning in Classroom Instruction.* New York: Macmillan, 1975. A clear, concise explanation of a system for individualizing instruction while insuring the mastery of prescribed objectives. Explains how it can be used to supplement conventional group methods of teaching. For "Some Criticisms of Mastery Learning," see the article bearing that title by Patrick Groff in *Today's Education,* November-December, 1974.

Clarizio, Harvey F. et al. eds. *Contemporary Issues in Educational Psychology.* 2d ed. Boston: Allyn and Bacon, 1974. Includes a number of articles related to the material dealt with in this chapter. Especially recommended are the articles in Unit IV, Measurement and Evaluation of Individual Differences, and Unit V, Educational Innovations, Instructional and Administrative Strategies.

Glatthorn, Allan A. *Alternatives in Education.* New York: Dodd Mead, 1975. A review of the more important developments in the movement toward alternative schools and programs. Discusses the need for and kinds of alternative approaches.

Gronlund, Norman E. *Individualizing Classroom Instruction.* Riverside, N.J.: Macmillan, 1974. A booklet of about 70 pages providing a concise description of several means of individualization including IPI and IGE.

Hull, Ronald E. "Selecting An Approach to Individualized Instruction." *Phi Delta Kappan,* November, 1973. Includes a description and evaluation

237

of "prepackaged" systems for individualization such as IPI, IGE, PLAN, and the Open Classroom concept.

Lesser, Gerald D., ed. *Psychology and Educational Practice.* Glenview, Ill.: Scott, Foresman, 1971. Among the articles in this anthology recommended for reading in connection with this chapter are those on matching instruction to student characteristics, educational implications of cognitive styles, teacher expectations and their effects upon children, and the nature and development of sex differences.

Sigel, Irving E., and Coop, Richard H. "Cognitive Style and Classroom Practice." In Richard H. Coop and Kinnard White, eds. *Psychological Concepts in the Classroom.* New York: Harper and Row, 1974. Reviews research on, and brings out the educational implications of, various learning styles, including analytic, relational-contextual, categorical-inferential, and field dependence-independence.

Sperry, Len, ed. *Learning Performance and Individual Differences.* Glenview, Ill.: Scott, Foresman, 1972. A book of readings including about 10 articles on each of the following: expectations, learning style, and instructional style. A good source of many points of view on the subject in one volume.

Index